JON

MW00874733

GRANDMA AND GRANDPA'S WISDOM FOR A HEALTHY AND PROSPEROUS LIFE

outskirts
press

Dedication

This book is dedicated to my best friend, who happens to be my most incredible wife, Danyel. You have brought so much happiness, unconditional love, friendship, and companionship into our family and my life. I have loved you since the first moment I saw you and plan to always, in all ways, love you more than any man has ever loved any woman.

This book is also dedicated to all the hardworking common sense people of the world who want to turn their common sense into an amazing life full of health and wealth beyond their dreams.

I'd also like to let my four amazing children—Nick, Andrew, Tyden, and Marcada—know how much I love and admire each of them. No father could be prouder of his children than I am of each of you. This world, and mine, is a better place because each of you is here on it. I know you will continue to bring great service to this world and demonstrate the brilliance of common sense and great added value in all you do.

As we start this journey together, please always know that who we are is our Creator's gift to us; who we become is our gift to him. Become great in all you are and do. Our Creator gave you everything you need to be all you can be. Without them ever knowing, this book is ultimately my grandparents' gift to you and this amazing world we are so blessed to live, serve, and prosper on.

Table of Contents

Pre-introduction

ONE DAY OUR youngest son, Tyden, and I were talking about my responsibilities as a father, a husband, a life coach, and a business consultant, and he asked, "How do you always know instantly and exactly what to say to your clients and us, in almost all situations?" I remember saying, "If everyone simply did what was right, they could advance much further, much faster, and ask much deeper questions, which would lead to much healthier and certainly wealthier lives. These deeper questions could lead to even more satisfaction in their lives in all areas and even more riches than they could imagine." Tyden said, "Everyone needs to know this, Dad. You should write a book for the world." At that exact moment, with the help of our seventeen-year-old son, I realized how I could have global impact on anyone wishing to know the answers to most of life's questions. I thought if every teenager—heck, every person on this planet could be exposed to the simple brilliance of my grandparents' wisdom, then this world would be a much more beautiful, healthy, prosperous, and safe place.

> *"The only impossible journey is the*
> *one you never begin."*
>
> *- Tony Robbins*

It seems rather simple but quite often I do not have to give deep thought to what my clients believe to be their hardest questions because I live by a few dozen simple rules/lessons my grandparents instilled in me during my teen years. These lessons seem to answer most, if not all, the questions one encounters on a daily basis in life and business. Yes, I completely understand that you still need technical, mechanical, financial, and other knowledge that would not appear to fit in the common sense of my grandparents' wisdom lessons. However, after you have completed reading this book and applied this information to whatever you do, you will do it much better and certainly live more prosperously. This information can positively affect everything from your relationships to your health and to your finances in ways you cannot imagine today.

Well, here they are, the simple rules from my amazing grandparents' wisdom to create an amazingly healthy and wealthy life full of love to you, yours, and hopefully the wonderful world we live in. I'd like to make it clear that I don't consider these Grandma and Grandpa rules exclusive to only my grandparents. In fact, many of these rules may be familiar to you and might even be related to concepts and rules you currently live by. We call them Grandma and Grandpa rules in the sense that they could easily be your grandparents' rules as well. Knowledge is not power until the knowing is added by doing. The next step will be your putting these rules into practice in your lives, day after day and year after year, and realizing how abundant your life can be. Shall we begin this journey together right now?

Introduction

DURING MY HIGH school years, I was blessed to live with my grandparents, Andy and Louise, who emigrated here from Italy. During this time, I was also crushed to the ground (while working at a lumberyard after school) by 480 pounds of lumber, which caused me great pain and to lose the use of both my legs, as well as losing bladder and bowel control. The amazing thing about this life-changing event was that it ended up being incredibly positive, even though it would take several years before I realized the blessings that came from this apparent tragedy. I now know that the days that break us are often the days that make us.

My parents divorced when I was very young and I have no memories, at least not good ones, of my father. My mom did the best she could to raise the four of us, but I'm convinced that we were much more than her two hands alone could manage.

It's funny how certain seemingly non-important moments in your childhood can change your life. One such moment that created a lifetime promise from me was being at the grocery store with my mom as a child and watching the look on the faces of the cashiers and the people around us when my mother handed over food stamps to pay for our groceries. As a child I promised God, and myself, I would never receive welfare from anyone for anything. I committed to always paying my way through life no matter what my circumstance.

Figuring out how I could make money so as to never need anyone's help consumed my waking thoughts. Shortly thereafter I started selling bubble gum in grade school to start building wealth. At the time you could buy a package of fifty pieces of gum for forty-nine cents, and I would sell each piece at school for three cents, making a dollar profit with every bag. Back then lunch milk cost two cents and often parents would give their children a nickel for milk. Thus, creating a three-cent surplus for me to capitalize on. Then as soon as I was old enough, I got a paper route and generated even more money. Then the general manager of the paper routes offered to take four or five of us out to sell newspaper subscriptions, so I did that and interestingly enough I was excited to sell subscriptions because that activity grew my paper route, which made me even more money. The obsession of never, ever receiving welfare was a great motivator to add value in all I did. I knew instinctually that I was put on this earth to add value to every experience I was involved in.

One day I was eating pizza and thought how great it would be to eat pizza every day and get paid for it. Our imaginations can be so powerful, positively or unfortunately negative, depending on our own use of them. Within two weeks of that thought, I was working at a fabulous pizza place, getting paid $1.00 an hour and eating all the pizza that was left over by the customers who chose not to take it home. I was soon making $20 to $30 per week at age fourteen and thought I was on top of the world financially. At that point of my life, as it is today, my goal in every job or earning endeavor was to outwork anyone near me in quality and quantity of production. I was not ever going to be on welfare!

A few months later I heard of a job at a local lumberyard that needed weekend morning help, and it paid $1.10 per hour. Next thing you know I was in high school working two jobs and making even more money than I knew people could make. Sometimes I'd clear over $100 per week with tips in the 1970s!

At the lumberyard, one of the most pivotal, life-changing events of my life occurred. Approximately 480 pounds of lumber slid off a forklift and crushed me to the ground. Hours later, I woke up in the hospital emergency room with no feeling below my belly button. I remember thinking two things: 1) Why me? This is terrible, and 2) I'm not going to spend the rest of my life in a wheelchair, wearing a diaper. It is amazing how powerful our thoughts can be. At that point in my life, I tended to only believe in God when things went well for me. I needed desperately to develop a much deeper faith.

Through some communication and lots of very quiet persuasion by an amazing nurse, with my grandpa, I was carried to his station wagon and brought to the office of a local chiropractor. THANK YOU to that particular nurse and all nurses for your service. It's true you really never know how far reaching one good deed or gesture will go. In the hours between the injury and being carried into the chiropractor's office, I had plenty of time to think about ways (negative ways) to not spend my life in a wheelchair, wearing a diaper.

The chiropractor did a bunch of tests and took x-rays of my back. To make a long story short, he made a specific chiropractic adjustment to my spine and I stood up! I stood up under my own power for the first time in nine hours! I proclaimed loudly to the chiropractor, my grandpa, and God that I was going to be a chiropractor. Then the real miracle happened—the chiropractor and my grandpa both gave me "the look." This was the exact same look that we received at the grocery store every time the food stamps came out. It was as if planning my demise for hours with no feeling in my legs wasn't enough; now I had received a specific chiropractic adjustment that brought my "dead" legs back to life, and "the look" said, "You are a street urchin, and there is no way you will ever become a doctor of any sort." Our thoughts are so powerful, and we must train ourselves to use them positively. I can honestly tell you "the look" that the chiropractor and my grandpa directed my way hurt much more than the stabbing back pain and not having working legs.

A few months later while I was at work at the pizza place, a customer observed my energy and work ethic and asked me how old I was. I exaggerated a bit and told him I was nineteen. He said with the excellent service that I had delivered to his wife and him, and after watching me out smile, out serve, and outwork everyone in the restaurant, he gave me his business card and said I should come work for him.

Next thing I knew, I was selling new cars at his Lincoln, Mercury, and Pontiac automobile dealership. A few months later, as a reward for being the top salesperson, I was driving a new black Firebird Trans Am and making "real" money. The positive looks people gave this actual seventeen-year-old, while I was driving that new Trans Am and spending all the money I was making, were magical. However, deep down inside I remembered the pain of "the look" from the chiropractor and my grandpa on that fateful day when I was crushed to the ground and lost the use of my legs and the promise I made to my grandpa, the chiropractor, and God. I KNEW I was going to be a chiropractor someday and help people the same way that chiropractor helped me.

As if growing up as a welfare kid, being raised by a single mother, and then losing the use of both of my legs for a day wasn't enough, the news came that I was going to have to go live with my grandparents.

My grandpa didn't like talking much, but everything he said always meant something. My grandma was the most unconditionally loving, happiest, and funniest person on the planet.

It wasn't long before their wisdom started getting pounded in my head by Grandpa (and I needed the impact) and happily inserted with love into my heart by Grandma.

It was a quick ten years later, and I was in practice as a chiropractor in Central California. Now some thirty-plus years later, I realize all the love, compassion, common sense, and wisdom I shared with my patients and family from all those years was 10 percent my doctorate degree and 90 percent the commonsense wisdom from Grandpa Andy and Grandma Louise.

My life has been so blessed in so many ways. It is true that the days that break you are truly the days that make you. I am extremely thankful to have been able to share that Grandma and Grandpa wisdom with so many patients, family, friends, and people over the years, to assist in creating blessings in their lives.

Today, as a life coach and business consultant to some of the top small businesses in the world, I hear daily that "you should write a book, so the world knows what you know!" This small book is an attempt to do so. I've always believed that I could have a major positive effect on the world, and maybe this is my vehicle. I believe that almost everything in this book you may have already heard or known. This is where I would like to share some Grandpa common sense. Knowing and doing are two completely different things that lead to completely different outcomes.

"Common sense is not so common."

- Voltaire

Here is the first not-so-secret secret I will share with you. Knowing means nothing without action. Knowledge is NOT POWER! In fact, knowledge doesn't mean much today when we can Google search anything we need to know about everything. However, when you take action on what you "know," now you have something. Knowledge combined with positive action is how to create positive outcomes and therefore develop wisdom.

"Nothing in this world can take the place of persistence. Talent will not: nothing is more common than unsuccessful men with talent. Genius will not; unrewarded genius is almost a proverb. Education will not: the world is full of educated derelicts. Persistence and determination alone are omnipotent."

- Calvin Coolidge

So, let's start there.

CHAPTER 1

"Success Loves Action"

ON ONE BEAUTIFUL sunny, summer Monday morning while driving to my office on a three-lane one-way street in the far-left lane, an impulse (feeling) went through me that felt like I should move out of that lane. In an instant the words that I'd heard from Grandma and Grandpa so many times— **"success loves action"**—flashed through my mind. I quickly visually made sure the center lane was clear and changed to the center lane at the exact same time as a car from my left skidded through the intersection, directly into that left lane I was just in. If I didn't take *immediate* action on "that feeling" (the right decision) or chose not to act upon it (the wrong decision) or worse yet sat in indecision (the worst decision) for even a second, I could have been in a terrible accident. In this particular incident the Grandma and Grandpa wisdom of "Success Loves Action" may have saved lives. For good people, like you, the quicker you take action on your "gut feelings" and your acquired knowledge, the more good thoughts and, more importantly, good, rapid, positive actions from you will become second nature. Thus, **"success loves action"** is a bit of Grandma and Grandpa wisdom to live by.

Throughout my life I've noticed that the most successful people are always in positive forward-moving action and/or taking action (and are very often hard workers). If you are a good person doing good things, you are wired for forward-moving progress in the direction of giving better and doing better. Here as our youngest son, Tyden, prepares to go to Marine bootcamp, I'll share with you the Marine Corps MARSOC motto: "Always Faithful, Always Forward." (The United States Marine Corps Forces Special Operations Command, MARSOC, is a component command of the United States Special Operations Command that comprises the Marine Corps' contribution to SOCOM. Its core capabilities are direct action, special reconnaissance, and foreign internal defense.) We utilize this thought process, with or without the actual words, in almost all our conversations. As long as you're always faithful to your mission and/or your life's purpose and you are moving forward, you'll do well. Very well.

Here you might be thinking that this piece of Grandma and Grandpa wisdom is okay, but I want to give more service or make a better product and make a lot more money. Maybe even millionaire money! Perfect, I have found, as I believe you will, that making good decisions, without hesitation or indecision, is one of the best things you can do to insure your prosperity.

> *"In any moment of decision, the best thing you can do is the right thing, the next best thing you can do is the wrong thing, and the worst thing you can do is the nothing."*
>
> *-Theodore Roosevelt*

What I'm getting at is if you are already a good person doing good things, you must trust that your natural state is good. This means that most, if not all, of your decisions will come from a state of good.

Therefore, trust yourself and make your decisions quicker than you have in the past. You're wired for good, so therefore who you seek counsel from (your coaches and mentors) as well as most of your decisions will be for the betterment of all involved.

As a rule, good people, such as you, doing good things don't make a lot of bad decisions. When you look back and think, *I made a bad decision*, it often wasn't a bad decision as much as it was indecision. I'm not saying good people can't make the wrong decision, but I believe they won't do it very often, if at all, if they live by this Grandma and Grandpa wisdom, **"Success loves action."**

The wrong decision made by good people, like you, can be used in our learning process to lead you to "fixing" that decision, which turns into a lesson that leads you to making a good decision, which leads to you making even more good decisions in your future. You are going to make mistakes, and if you make them once and learn from them, that's truly how you learn. However, if we continually make the same mistakes over and over again, we are forming habits of bad decisions. Today, for example, our youngest son was actually proofreading this chapter when he ran upstairs and put a dirty dish in the sink and came down to finish helping me. A few minutes later I noticed he put that dirty dish in the sink, which his mother had left very clean prior to going to town. I asked him why he left that dirty dish there versus rinsing it out and completing his task in one movement—instead of aggravating the Grandma and Grandpa rule of "Cleanliness is next to Godliness." He said: "Yes, I know I should have done it before being barked at." I simply asked which rule we live by that would have circumvented the entire conversation, and he instantly said: **"Success Loves Action,"** the chapter we were proofreading.

This incident may seem small, but if we live by another Grandma and Grandpa rule—"As you do one thing is how you do all things"— which we do, I asked how this would be different than going out on patrol and forgetting to bring ammo. Everything we do may not appear, or actually ever lead, to a life-or-death decision, but hopefully he learned that day, and you can see how much easier your decisions could be made living by a set of Grandma and Grandpa rules. Imagine eventually doing almost everything you have to do the right way, with little to no indecision, because you had a clear set of rules for life as opposed to having to ask yourself every time you had to make any decision, "What should I do?"

I believe people who are often indecisive have not enjoyed the thrill of what comes from doing the right thing. Or they've made the wrong decision before and are fearful of making more wrong decisions, and consequentially feel safer doing nothing. I believe a good number of really good people, like you, reading this book are so afraid of doing things wrong that they never create a chance to do something right. Stop right now and trust that you are a good person doing good things, and the more you trust in our Creator, these Grandma and Grandpa rules, and yourself, the more often you'll make the right decisions. You have to have faith. I believe reading this book is a great decision on your part. I believe knowing the content of this book is an even better decision on your part. But the best decision I believe you can make is taking positive action on all the Grandma and Grandpa wisdom you are about to live by.

The Bible tells us over and over again that where there is faith, there is no need. Grandpa repeatedly told me that **"Success Loves Action,"** and that meant "Get moving, boy."

Have supreme faith in that greater power which we call God and/ or our Creator. Have faith in yourself, that you are a good person, doing good things, and take positive actions on all of the thoughts that flow through you. After all, **"Success Loves Action."**

Thank you God, Grandma and Grandpa!

CHAPTER 2

"Anything Worth Doing Is Worth Doing Well"

LAST YEAR ON the Wednesday evening before Thanksgiving, I developed intense mouth pain. That pain was so bad that being thankful for anything other than pain reduction, any eating and any watching football were clearly not going to be possible for days. I recalled fifteen years prior when that exact area of my mouth hurt just as bad and led to a root canal and crown. Looking back, I can say with certainty that the original crown never fit right, often collected a lot of food particles, and ached off and on for fifteen years. I made the mistake of putting up with it and thinking this must be how crowns and root canals are. I also remember thinking, *how can this possibly hurt this bad?* At the time the dentist said: "Some pain is physical, and some pain is mental, but nothing hurts like dental." Man, oh man, was he right. I had to do something, so I called my dental office late Wednesday night. I was so blessed to have a dentist who returned my after-hours call within minutes. She asked important diagnostic questions, listened to me describe my predicament, and instantly wrote a prescription for the needed antibiotics and advised I should pick up some over-the-counter pain medication. The antibiotics kicked in about six hours later, and the pain became tolerable for the weekend until I could get in to see her on Monday.

On Monday, after a dental examination and x-rays, she determined that I had a failed root canal that needed surgical extraction. Long story short I feel that something was not done correctly on the original procedure, even if that was on my part by not complaining. This led to fifteen years of problems. And this eventually led to another year of multiple oral surgical procedures, including placing cadaver bone in the hole left by the extraction. This led to a new crown installation, which my current dentist sized several times for a perfect fit. I am not a dentist, but I believe that when a root canal and crown are done correctly, food doesn't have to pack in between the crown, and you don't have to ache for years.

My point is that if the original procedure had been fitted correctly, I would have had a lot less suffering. This is exactly why I live by the Grandma and Grandpa rule "Anything worth doing is worth doing well." How many times have we heard or thought this? If we look back to the previous chapter and add both of these first two Grandma and Grandpa wisdoms—"Success loves action" and "Anything worth doing is worth doing well"—to the dirty plate in the clean sink, we can see how easily both these rules could have helped avoid wasted time, aggravation, and energy.

Oftentimes, Grandpa's words of wisdom were delivered with the help of Pete and Re-Pete. You see, Grandpa's right hand was respectfully called Pete, and I'll bet you already figured out that his left hand was known as Re-Pete. I promise you at that stage of my life, Pete and Re-Pete's impact on me positively changed and most likely saved my life.

The lessons often started out something like this: Grandpa and Grandma would give me an assignment like taking out the garbage. Simple, right? You take the brown paper garbage bag out from under the sink, you replace it with a new bag in the now washed-out and dried container, and then you take the full garbage bag outside and put it in the big garbage bin that goes out to the curb on Thursday.

Some things are not as easy as you would think, because of all the variables. Did the container have any debris or stuff left in it? Did you wash and dry the container completely? Did you replace the container fast enough for Grandpa? Did you leave any drips in your path from the kitchen to the big bin? Did you place the full garbage bag in the right spot in the big bin? Did you replace the big bin top properly?

"Make your decisions for what is right not expedient, and wash your mind of all compromise."
-B.J. Palmer, The Developer of Chiropractic

Let's say that you noticed the garbage had to be taken out before you were told to do it. Let's also say that you actually looked into the container prior to putting a new bag in it, and there was not any debris or stuff left in it, but you washed and dried it out anyway. Then you didn't even spill a drop of anything on your journey from the kitchen to the big garbage bin. Even though you have done a fantastic job up to this point, there is always something more you can do or add to any situation. Here comes the lesson—get ready!

Grandpa calls you outside and whacks you with Pete and tells you, **"Anything worth doing is worth doing well!"** You get your bearings only to find out that after all the good you did, you forgot to put the big bin top on properly, and the smell escaping from the poorly replaced lid will attract raccoons, and then the garbage will be everywhere. This will cause so much more work than if done properly. Everything would be so much better if you simply remembered, **"Anything worth doing is worth doing well!"**

Over the four years of living with my grandma and grandpa, I'll bet I heard this life lesson from them hundreds of times, and unfortunately, Re-Pete was involved often.

To this day I am so thankful for this life lesson as a father, as a doctor, as a husband, and as a man. I'll bet that I say this to myself dozens of times per week: **"Anything worth doing is worth doing well."** I can be talking to one of my children and they might be talking about athletics, academics, or just about anything, and the answer often is **"Anything worth doing is worth doing well!"** Sometimes they say, "You're right, thanks!" and sometimes they roll their eyes. Anytime a patient wanted to direct their care into a direction that was not the best for them, I'd counter with **"Anything worth doing is worth doing well!"** They'd usually agree and thank me. When my wife and I discuss just about anything, we end up saying, **"Anything worth doing is worth doing well!"** Whether I'm mending a fence on the ranch or talking about financial decisions that could impact a family for generations, I know, **"Anything worth doing is worth doing well."** I've even added to that with my children and created the new and improved Grandma and Grandpa rule: "Anything worth doing is worth doing exceptionally well." You see, anything and everything can be improved upon.

Thank you God, Grandma, Grandpa, Pete and Re-Pete, for your timeless rules and wisdom!

CHAPTER 3

"Do unto others as you would want them to do unto you."

I GREW UP without ever meeting my father, and I regularly wished that I had a father in my life who could teach me about doing the right things to advance my life without so many painful lessons—lessons I had to learn on my own until I was blessed enough to move in with my grandparents. Prior to moving in with my grandparents, I was invited to a father/son Boy Scout soapbox derby event that really pounded one of these hard-earned lessons home for me. I had just been invited to join the Boy Scouts and received a plastic bag with four nails, four wheels, and a balsa-wood block in it. This package, for those lucky enough to have a dad at home who could share common knowledge, contained the basic beginning parts necessary for building a sleek, beautiful, and oh so importantly fast soapbox car. You can imagine my surprise, and total embarrassment, on the day of the big derby when I showed up with the four nails pounded through the four wheels into the untrimmed, unpainted, and totally unfinished balsa block. Not to mention the fact that the nails were pounded in so tightly that the wheels would not even spin on my derby car.

As the fifty or so Boy Scouts' derby cars were unveiled one by one and prepared to race down the track. When they got to mine, not only did the announcer burst into laughter but everyone in attendance did as well upon seeing my unfinished car, which would not even roll downhill. I was so embarrassed that I ran out of the building and never returned to the Boy Scouts.

Now to this day I believe the Boy Scouts of America is a great group with a great cause; however, that mortally embarrassing moment created a hard-earned lesson for me that I'll never forget. I absolutely knew from that moment on that I would never wish upon anyone that much public embarrassment. Before I was even taught this Grandma and Grandpa rule and Biblical quote, **"Do unto others as you would want them to do unto you,"** I would attempt to live by it.

On a much brighter note, every time I was confronted with a decision that involved others, I never had to think about what to do—I simply treated others exactly as I would want to be treated in that particular situation. When I graduated from the Palmer College of Chiropractic several years ago and was about to start my practice, living by this Grandma and Grandpa rule and well-known Biblical quote created massive abundance in my heart and bank account. Upon starting my own clinic, I was faced with the question of which type of practice I should develop. Would my practice be centered around the concepts of relief care or would I pursue the much less traveled path of spinal corrective care? I instantly knew that a spinal corrective care chiropractor had changed my life and thought that if everyone knew what I knew about correction versus relief care, there would be no question: They would want corrective care versus relief care every time.

Before starting my clinic, I consulted dozens of established chiropractors who for the most part said, "People want a quick fix that's inexpensive and often covered by insurance, rather than a long, drawn-out corrective care process that would most certainly not be covered by insurance and could cost thousands of dollars and take months to years." I knew what I would want if I was a patient with that choice, and thus, I set out on a course of developing corrective care for patients who came to my clinics and the clinics of those I trained in corrective care. I knew in my heart that I was going to live by this piece of Grandma and Grandpa wisdom: **"Do unto others as you would want them to do unto you."**

This is a command based on the words of Jesus in the Sermon on the Mount: "All things whatsoever ye would that man should do to you, do ye even so to them." The World English Bible translates this passage as: "Therefore, whatever you desire for men to do to you, you shall also do to them; for this is the law and the prophets."

This command was driven home within weeks of moving in with Grandma and Grandpa. Yes, Pete got into the deep driving home part of this message as well. You probably remember Pete was Grandpa's right hand. You see, we were going to the grocery store, and during the pushing of the cart ritual, apparently, I veered into the other lane a bit, and *whack*, Pete caught me off guard in the back of the head. Grandpa said, "Stay on your side of the aisle! How would you like it if someone came across your side and forced you to pull over?" Simultaneously Grandpa said while Pete reiterated, **"Do unto others as you would have them do unto you.** It even says so in the Bible!"

> *"You can get anything in life you want*
> *if you'll just help enough other people*
> *get what they want."*
>
> *- Zig Ziglar*

I'm sure there were dozens, if not multiple dozens of other times Grandpa and sometimes Pete drove that lesson home during my teen years. The beauty of Grandpa and Pete's anchoring of this command is that still to this day, on any business deal, the reason I can create excellent opportunities for all is because I always think, *how can I make this opportunity excellent for all involved?* Heck, even last week I parked our Yukon XL in a great spot at the mall, only to notice the rear end was sticking out farther than seemed best for those turning in to the lane I was in. I asked my wife and daughter to go ahead; I was going to find a better spot. Our daughter, Marcada, looked at me and said, "They don't get better than the first spot in the first row, do they?" I replied, "Maybe not for us, but if I move out about ten spots, it will be much easier on the dozens who try to go down this row while we're shopping." You know it is always best to **"Do unto others as you would want them to do unto you,"**

As I watch people cutting in line, not obeying the right-of-way rule at stop signs, and seldom holding doors for the next person, I wonder how much better this world could be if we simply treated each other the way we wished to be treated?

Thank you God, Grandma, Grandpa, Pete and Re-Pete, for another timeless and positively life-changing lesson.

CHAPTER 4

"What you think about, you talk about, and eventually you bring about."

THE POSITIVE TRAINING of your mind is so simple for some to do, and it is often just as simple for others not to do. After coaching hundreds of people toward their next level of business and life success, I have noticed a trend of success. This trend will seem ridiculously simple, so get ready. This simple observation I've made is the ease that successful people have in saying and seeing the positive versus the ease struggling people have in saying and seeing the negative. I'll take it one step further and tell you that if after reading the previous sentence your instant response is "Of course you have to ask the positive questions and think the positive thoughts," there is a good chance your journey of growth and financial abundance will be easier. If your instant response was something like "That's ridiculous; nothing can be that simple" or "Nothing in business or life is that easy," there is a good chance your journey of growth and financial abundance will be much more difficult unless you change your thoughts to positive ones. This little test can instantly determine where your thoughts are at this moment. Yes, you can change your thoughts and change your outcome, or you can argue it and stay exactly where you are. It's your choice—always has been and always will be.

Often what we think about becomes what we talk about, and eventually that is what we bring about in our businesses, in our jobs, and in our lives. When consulting a person who is having a tough go in their current situation, a simple question can often lead to determining what their obstacle is. I can ask something as simple as "What is the main objective of your business?" If they answer with something like "I want to be able to pay the bills without all the stress associated with managing people," this simple response reveals three key things in their thought process:

1) Their focus is more on getting by (simply paying the bills) than prospering.
2) They focus on the stress of their business or their job more than the joy.
3) They feel there is more difficulty in managing people than the great experience of sharing their knowledge with others.

If they answer something like "I want to grow my business 20 percent and train my staff to give our customers an even better experience," this simple response reveals three key things in their thought process:

1) Their focus is on growing and prospering.
2) They enjoy their job or owning and running their business.
3) They feel managing people to their full potential can create a great experience of sharing their knowledge with others.

Yesterday during my consulting calls, I tested this on two clients who are at two different extremes on the enjoying life and financial spectrum by asking one question: "What is your main goal for your business next year?"

The doctor who runs four very successful clinics, works three mornings per week in, and on, his clinics, has an amazing marriage with his college sweetheart, and has three amazing children said without hesitation: "We are going to increase new patient admission 30 percent this next year by adding three more doctors. With these additional doctors and the four additional support staff we'll need, we will increase our overall patient retention by 25 percent, and the overall positive patient experience will be improved exponentially. By creating this next level of service for our patients, we will be employing seven additional people, increasing overall staff pay, increasing staff bonuses, and creating even more time off for our employees than anyone in our profession. And the bottom line will be an increase in revenue of over $1,450,000 for our organization. I will cut my hours 60 percent and start working *on* my business, and no longer *in* my business, one morning per week."

The other doctor is very new to our coaching program. He runs a struggling clinic, works over forty-five hours per week in his clinic, and according to him has a "pretty good marriage even though there is more arguing than laughing and two teenage children who are having a tough time getting by in high school and at home," said after a lot of hemming and hawing. "If I could at least be able to pay some of my last three years' back taxes, I think everything wouldn't be so terrible."

Grandma was so intuitive, and no matter what was happening, she could make me laugh. Grandma's process of teaching was never to lash out physically. Oh no, she was much better at making me feel embarrassed and getting me to laugh on the outside, while crying on the inside. In fact, after about six months of living with Grandma and Grandpa, I outwardly appeared to fear Grandpa and Pete, while I inwardly laughed that the physical impacts didn't really hurt me. However, when Grandma would say something like "If you're proud of being sent home from school for fighting, we all will be," she was sarcastically saying that she was proud of me when she obviously wasn't, directing me to think more and be better in all of my actions. And as she went on with her housework, I ached inside to know I had done anything that would ever hurt her in any way.

In the first few months with Grandma and Grandpa, I got into a lot of trouble in school, out of school, and pretty much on a daily basis. Apparently, I had issues with being raised without a father figure, and to this day I have no idea how I would have turned out without Grandma, Grandpa, and of course Pete. Thank you, Grandma, Grandpa, and Pete. Without you and your lessons, I'm sure I would not have turned out to help thousands of people during my life and hopefully still help thousands, if not tens of thousands, with this book.

Back to this chapter's title: **"What you think about, you talk about, and eventually you bring about."** Grandma would catch me thinking about something (and I'm sure somehow, she knew it wasn't good) and say, "What wonderful things are going through your head right now?" There I was, thinking about fighting someone at school tomorrow or one of the many evils thoughts that would go through my head at that time in my life, and when Grandma would simply ask me a positive question, somehow it would change my thoughts into something positive. I'd quickly, not wanting to ever hurt her feelings, say something like "I'm thinking about what I need to do to get a good grade on my history test tomorrow." She'd say, "I'm sure you'll figure it out. You're such a good boy!"

Thoughts in the wind determine your course,
Steering your life for better or worse.
If you dwell on thoughts that are petty and unkind,
Pain will follow you as the ox's plough—behind.
But dwell on thoughts that are noble and pure,
And joy will follow as your shadow sure.

-Adapted from a saying of the Buddha

Pretty soon, the constant reminders from Grandpa and Pete that I would never amount to much drove something inside of me to never quit at anything. And I knew I would never need welfare from anyone. Even more importantly, the constant good thoughts and unconditional love that Grandma "laughed" into me changed my bad thoughts into good thoughts. I kid you not, when I first moved in with Grandma and Grandpa, I KNEW I was not ever going to be the kind of person who did good things and succeeded in life. Then within a few years of their direction, my thoughts turned 180 degrees, and I knew I was put on earth to help people and do good things!

Later in my life I came upon two amazing books that helped me see the true brilliance in thinking positively. One was the Bible, where throughout its entirety, it says where there is hope, there is no need, and specifically Proverbs, chapter 23, verse 7: "As a man thinketh in his heart, so is he." The second book, written by James Allen, is *As a Man Thinketh*. This entire book is a goldmine of examples of why what we think about, we talk about, and we eventually bring about.

As James Allen said in his book, "The mind is like a garden which can be cultivated or allowed to run wild. Either way, it will bring forth results. If seeds of intelligent thought are planted and nurtured, they will grow until a healthful harvest. If the garden is left to chance, weeds' seeds will blow in, take root, and flourish producing nothing of use."

Have you ever had something go not the way you intended and said, "How else could this possibly get worse?" And then it gets worse. From this lesson I realized I should never focus on what could get worse because then that is what you are setting your sights for. Instead I learned to be thankful of my wins, and equally thankful of my lessons learned from losses. From that point on, no matter the outcome positive or negative, I'd ask, "What else could go right or how could this get better?"

Imagine if everyone in your town did a thirty-day discipline of only thinking good thoughts and doing good deeds! I'll bet it would be such a great month that the powers that be would make a law demanding that everyone was only allowed to think good thoughts and do good deeds.

Gandhi once said, "Be the change you wish for in the world." For thirty days do you think you could only think positive thoughts and only say positive words? I'll tell you right now it will change your life and our world. It is often true that **"what you think about, you talk about, and eventually you bring about."**

Thank you God, Grandma, Grandpa, Pete, Re-Pete and all involved who changed my stinking thinking into an amazing life of positive and prosperous thoughts.

CHAPTER 5

"If you're going to expect anything from anyone, you must inspect everything from everyone."

SO MANY TIMES, while observing and studying my own businesses, the businesses of others, or my life, as well as others' lives, I've found that no one ever seems to be as interested in another person's success as much as that individual. I've been blessed to be surrounded by people who have helped me create the abundance of health, love, and financial prosperity I enjoy, yet it still seems as if I have to keep an eye on all I'm responsible for. I'm not saying micromanaging is the answer. However, I do believe no one, other than you, will ever care as much about your well-being, happiness, or success as you.

Sometimes this responsibility can be as simple as walking into a room in your house and noticing a light that was left on, even though no one is in the room. You might find yourself saying, "Who cares about wasting electricity?" The person paying the bill and only the person paying the bill! I'll bet a lot of good parents and/or business owners would search for the perpetrator of this crime and bring them to the room and ask, "Any idea who left this light on?" I'll bet it's someone who doesn't pay the electrical bill! Sometimes this example can be a lot harder to notice or a lot more expensive to fix.

Example #1: You're receiving service from a person who has "a job" serving versus receiving service from a server who loves their job. Most of us have experienced this. You walk into a restaurant and get an okay greeting and are directed to a table. Then after a few too many minutes, a server walks up who appears to not be enjoying their day or job and asks, "Are you guys ready to order?" You order, you wait and wait, and eventually your food comes, and it is placed in front of you with the question "Did you order the chicken?" As if that server didn't even take the order. Whether the food is good, great, or okay, there is something in that experience that causes you to never return to that business. Then in some amount of time, often a very short period of time, the business closes and the staff is unemployed and searching for another job. Meanwhile the poorly performing server is explaining to everyone who will listen how customers didn't tip, how difficult it was serving, and how hard it is looking for another job. Because of this underperforming employee, the restaurant's entire staff is now suffering simply because the owner did not inspect and direct the quality of this employee's work.

Example #2: You're receiving service from a person who loves their job and the positive experiences that go with it. Whether it's a part-time or career server, if they are well trained in the fine points of serving, they will know the better the service, the better the customers' experience. This will eventually lead to a bigger overall bill and a better tip. One night, you walk into a restaurant and someone cheerfully greets you with a big smile and says, "I have the perfect table for the two of you right over here. Please come with me." Then prior to seating you he asks, "Is this table perfect for both of you tonight?" You're already blown away by the greeting, the energy, and the direction, and you'll most likely say, "Thank you, this is perfect." Then as he hands you the menu, he might say something like "If you're interested, the chef's special tonight is her mother's secret recipe lasagna. And when I say secret, she won't even tell us what's in it, but I can tell you there's a lot of love in it and it is fantastic! It's our most complimented dish. And if paired with our incredible house Chianti, which is from Napa, you will have an amazing dinner experience tonight. And if by chance you're feeling like something different, every single item on our menu is homemade and fantastic! Can I get you both some sparkling water and maybe some wine or a cocktail while you're exploring our menu?" Of course, one or both of you orders the lasagna, and your experience is already one you want to positively share with others. A few minutes after your order has been placed, your server returns with that genuine smile, your sparkling water, and your wine. Upon setting your wine in front of you, he says, "Please taste it and make sure it's perfect for you." And of course, it is. Very shortly your entrees arrive, delivered with that same incredible energy and the genuine warmth of your server. The server comes back to ask if everything is perfect for you and brings you more sparkling water while asking, "Can I bring you another glass of wine?" And of course, you both order more wine and eventually order the incredible desserts your server thought would be a perfect complement with your after-dinner freshly brewed coffee. Then, often in a short period of time, the business gets amazing reviews and is booked full weeks in advance. The entire staff are some of the highest paid in their industry (insurance benefits included) and becoming better every day because everyone wants to work in that amazing place, and the amazing server is explaining to everyone who will listen how they cannot believe how much people tip and how quickly they were promoted to manager and eventually co-owner.

The reason I could share this story so vividly is because both examples occurred for my wife and me in the same restaurant. The second example occurred several times first for us; we loved going to that place so much, we told lots of people how great the restaurant was, and eventually we'd have to call weeks in advance to get in. The original owners had their fingers, thoughts, and love in every aspect of that business, so it thrived. The original owners cared about every aspect of their business and apparently knew Grandma and Grandpa's rule: "**If you're going to expect anything from anyone, you must inspect everything from everyone.**" Then the original owners sold out to the new owners, and the first example occurred once for us, we never returned, and they closed their doors within fourteen months. The new owners counted on their employees to do their jobs without much direction or inspection and more than likely lost everything they had.

Early in my days with Grandma and Grandpa, I realized part of my duty was to understand what they were thinking, but more importantly to understand what they were saying. Making Grandpa mad really made this task complicated. You see, when Grandpa was upset, he spoke in Italian (which I didn't understand), or he simply let Pete, his right hand, do the communicating. However, it appeared shortly after I moved in with them that he learned a third way of communicating: stuttering, which always led him to turn over communication to Pete. He would get so mad at me, he would stutter, and no matter how funny it seemed, I knew I should not laugh.

Once Grandpa handed me a set of hand pruners and instructed me to trim his prized lilac bushes that separated his yard from the neighbors. He then left for a round of golf with his buddies.

I knew that he trimmed them at exactly six feet. I also knew he had to do that trimming from a ladder with outstretched arms with the hand pruners, and he could easily fall and be injured. I figured that to make the process safer, we could eliminate the ladder and trim them at four feet. I knew this would be easier simply by eliminating the danger of falling from the ladder, and instead of having to trim the bushes every two to three weeks in the summer, we could go six to ten weeks before they got over six feet. I went at this project knowing that Grandpa would be so proud of my genius pruning job when he returned from his golf game that there would be some amazing reward coming my way.

> ***"The only true wisdom is in knowing***
> ***you know nothing."***
>
> -*Socrates*

About an hour into my pruning job, Grandma came out and said, "Grandpa's going to kill us. What have you done?" I went on to explain how smart I was to cut the lilacs at four feet versus six feet. I talked about the ease of pruning and most importantly the safety of working from the ground versus leaning from the ladder. As usual, Grandma was all in and in fact praised me for the thought that I had put into this assignment. Now two of us were convinced that this was a major breakthrough in pruning Grandpa's purple and white lilacs. We both knew he would be proud of me. I cleaned the yard and had all of the trimmings out to the street and observed my work from several angles to make sure it was perfect.

I must have fallen asleep in the breezeway, dreaming about how proud Grandpa would be of me, when I woke up to him screaming and stuttering in Italian, and things being thrown around in the garage. Grandpa found me and proceeded to drag me out to my masterpiece and his nightmare. When the hollering was over, and Pete said a few things, I realized that Grandpa wanted those bushes at six feet so he couldn't see the neighbors and they couldn't see us. I had wrecked that, and it would take most of the summer for the bushes to grow back.

Grandma and Grandpa discussed this several times over the next eight weeks, and once I remember Grandma saying, "You know he's a boy and **if you are going to expect anything from anyone, you must inspect everything from everyone."**

Years later I realize that I have managed my children, employees, and companies exactly that way. I have spent most of my adult life giving specific directions to specific people on a specific job and then checking in on their progress. I'm not talking about micromanaging as much as hiring or assigning the right people to the right jobs and attempting to give them the right amount of direction. This is always followed by a thorough inspection.

I encourage you to try this at home and at work, to see if your over-all results improve. I'm sure your spouse and your children are worth it, and I'll bet your career/job is worth it as well. After all, anything worth doing is worth doing well. You know: **"If you're going to expect any-thing from anyone, you must inspect everything from everyone."**

Thank you God, Grandma, Grandpa, Pete and Re-Pete and all the masterful servers out there in all the businesses who make all the difference in those businesses.

CHAPTER 6

"Reputation, reputation, reputation—that's all you've got."

ANYONE WHO KNOWS anything about real estate can tell you without hesitation the three most important rules of real estate are location, location, location—a good rule to live by if you choose to purchase real estate, whether you are picking a location for your home or for your business. One of my original business and life coaches in the 1980s, Dr. Wayne Pack, used to tell me, "As a doctor you have two things in your control: the decisions you make for your patients' health and your reputation. NEVER mess up either of those, EVER!" It was such a blessing to have a doctor with a thirty-plus-year career mentoring and directing me at that time in my career and life. I could never thank him enough or put a price on his sharing of wisdom. At some point during my associateship with Dr. Pack, I vividly remember asking him, "How do you create a really good reputation?" In between his chuckles he said, "Great question." That was all he said before walking away to see another patient, and I realized the answer was in the question.

From that day forward, whenever a patient would compliment the care they received in our clinic, my staff and I would say, "Thank you very much for your kind words. We work very hard to be our very best for you. Please continue to tell your friends about how good we are." At the beginning of my practice career in the 1980s, I saw the writing on the wall about insurance and chose to avoid it. I decided we would give our patients the care they *actually needed* and charge them a fair price for it versus being told by an insurance company how much care they thought the patient needed. It wasn't but a few months later when new patients started coming into our office saying, "Dr. Baker, I was told that your office care was very good, but I'm not sure we can afford to come here." That's when I would say something like "I completely understand but usually very good and expensive go hand in hand." That's when I decided our new response and reputation would be "We're very good and expensive." Within a year, and for the next thirty-plus years, our reputation grew—and grew exponentially. Four out of five new patients would come to our clinic and say, "I heard your care was very good and you're expensive." We trained ourselves to say, "Yes, the two often go hand in hand and we'll take great care of you." When everyone else in health care was complaining about how the insurance companies made it so hard to give quality care with the reduced fees paid, we were serving more and more people quality care and also opened nine more clinics before 1993, utilizing our model. I guess if you're going to have a reputation, it should be one you're very proud of. "Very good and expensive" sounds much better to me than "He's okay and accepts your insurance."

My grandfather had a third-grade education when he came to this country from Palermo, Sicily, on a ship. He initially arrived at Ellis Island and some years later claimed residence in Rockford, Illinois. Grandma and her twelve other sisters all lived in Rockford as well. In the 1970s, when I moved in with my grandparents, it was a weekly Sunday ritual for all the ladies to prepare a magnificent meal to feed the entire family. These events were more often than not held at my godfather, Uncle Tony's, house. All the Italian men in our family took great pride in their immaculate homes and gardens, but Uncle Tony's was the most impeccably kept home with the best garden of all. His house was large, and he had the most amazing yard, but his real source of pride came from his garden, which was beautiful, had every vegetable you could imagine, and was without any trace of weeds.

Back then our family ritual was for the ladies to cook, drink homemade red wine, laugh, and teach the younger girls the fine art of being an Italian woman. The men would sit in woven lawn chairs, near their gardens, and tell stories while drinking the same "dago red" as they called it. The boys would sit on the ground, just outside the circle of wisdom, listen to the life lessons, and sneak sips of the "dago red" when no one was watching.

On one of these beautiful Sunday events, which occurred at about 11:30 a.m. (because Catholic mass was let out at 11:00 a.m.), I remember my uncle Sam telling the story of real estate. As he got to the good part, he leaned in and said, "The most important things you all need to know about real estate are location, location, and location!" As everyone sat in awe, Grandpa leaned in and said, "Exactly like the three most important things you all need to know about being a man: **reputation, reputation, and reputation—that's all you've got!**" And, of course, right before the third reputation was shared, Pete knocked me over backward and spilled Grandpa's wine that I thought I was sneaking. Pete delivered Grandpa's message exactly as I must have needed it; however, Grandpa wanted to make sure I got it.

I remember him saying, "Do you want to be known as a thief?" Then, just to lock in the lesson, "Do you want to be a drunk like your father?"

I realize today people may think that was abuse, but I've got to tell you, it was the blessing I needed at that time to lock in another priceless lesson. Thank you, God, Grandpa, and Pete.

> *"Reputation is what men and women think of us.*
> *Character is what God and angels know of us."*
>
> *-Thomas Paine*

From that moment, whenever I felt like quitting anything, I wouldn't, because I didn't want a reputation as a quitter. Anytime I thought drinking was going to solve a problem, I wouldn't, because I never wanted the reputation as a drunk. I'm not saying I didn't slip a few times in my life. Interestingly enough, I was with some close friends several years ago, and we were having the time of our lives in Maui. After a day of boogie boarding, telling stories, and over drinking on the beach, I let the alcohol decide that beach MMA was a good idea. After several rounds there were beach chairs all over, a few bloody faces, lots of bruised friends, an empty bottle of vodka, and some very disappointed wives. Later that evening (or the next day), my wife explained to me, "These people look up to you for everything; their families count on your direction; their businesses rely on you. **Reputation, reputation, and reputation—that's all you've got.** Please don't create a reputation as displayed yesterday!" The pain of embarrassing my wife was actually sharper than the bruises from the MMA event, and I can tell you that stopped right then and there for all of us.

In practice, whether because of lack of knowledge or lack of money, patients would sometimes say, "Can we take a shortcut with my care plan?" I'd instantly say, "In this office we have two things: your health and my reputation, and I'll never risk either." Thank you so much Grandma, Grandpa, and Pete. After all, in life you really only have three things…**reputation, reputation, and reputation—that's all you've got.**

Thank you God, Grandma, Grandpa, Dr. Wayne Pack, Pete and Re-Pete for the endless possibilities you have created by your blessings and wisdom.

CHAPTER 7

"Common sense is not so common."

AS A STUDENT at the Palmer College of Chiropractic in Davenport, Iowa, in the early 1980s, I was intrigued by the wealth of many of the European students. A good number of them took elaborate vacations during summer, winter, and spring breaks, and a few even drove high-end European cars. As I investigated this phenomenon, I discovered that the currency exchange at the time was 3.2 Deutsche Marks to the dollar. Curiously as I asked more and more of the European students about this exchange rate, they were happy to explain to me that for every 3.2 Deutsche Marks they brought to America, they received one of our dollars. This little bit of research revealed that the European students came from even more wealth than I had imagined and were paying three dollars of their money to buy one dollar of our money. The exchange rate information fascinated me. I wondered if it could be turned around in a way that I could buy three dollars of their money for one dollar of our money. It sure seemed like the reversal of currency exchange could be an excellent avenue of prosperity for me. I thought that if I reversed this currency exchange rate in my favor, I could buy

3.2 dollars of product in Europe for one American dollar, get it shipped here, and make three times my money.

What could I possibly buy in Europe, without actually going there, that people would want to buy from me? How would I possibly get it here? I was talking to my friend and classmate, Ole from Denmark, about it, and the answer was right in front of me. His bright red Porsche 911. It seemed so simple and interesting. The process seemed to be common sense to me. When the European students would go home for their holiday break, I would tell them the exact type of car to purchase that I thought would be easy to resell. Usually that was a two- to three-year-old Porsche 911 or Mercedes 420 sedan. When they located the car, I would wire the money to the seller and a few hundred dollars to the student who located the car as a finder's fee. I'd put an insurance binder on the car, and the student would have a nice vehicle to drive during their break and extra money in their pockets. When their break was over, they would drive the newly purchased vehicle to the shipping dock in their country, and I would prearrange the shipping of the car to New Jersey. When notification came that the car or cars were at the docks in America, I would gather as many drivers, who were college friends, as needed. I'd fly them, all expenses paid plus a bit extra, to the East Coast to pick up the cars, and we would cannonball run back to Iowa. Then I would have the cars DOT certified (Department of Transportation) and place ads to sell them in the surrounding big cities of Des Moines and Chicago. Simply put, I'd get roughly $32,000 in European product for $10,000, ship the car from Europe to New Jersey for about $700, pay students a few hundred dollars to drive the vehicles to Iowa, spend about $600 more for DOT certifications, and finally sell the vehicles for about $29,000. Everyone won, from the sellers of the vehicles, to the people who in the end purchased the vehicles and everyone in between. This entire process seemed to be common sense and a bit of good luck. Not to mention that this business venture allowed me to leave graduate school with no student loans and a box full of money to start my professional career.

It was easy realizing my grandfather worked incredibly hard to build his life in America because he told me of his struggles daily. He told me of the dedication it took to own a home and live the American Dream. When he just about had his home paid off, and his life was supposed to get easier for him and Grandma, they took me in. Talk about a disruption of your dreams. Imagine how much freedom my grandparents sacrificed by taking in a teenager with a big chip on his shoulder. Imagine the difficulty of getting on a boat as a child and traveling across the Atlantic Ocean only to be processed at Ellis Island while not even being able to speak the English language. Then after all that working laborious jobs, buying a home, raising a child, and finally paying off that home, and just when the celebration is about to start, you take on a troubled teen. No thanks!

I'm approaching sixty years of age and still thank my grandparents daily in my prayers for their sacrificial love and affection. And yes, I thank Pete from time to time, and now laugh when I think about how dense I must have been to need Re-Pete to step in occasionally to help guide me.

My grandfather had a third-grade school education, but I believe he had his master's degree in life and common sense. It always seemed, and still does, that for being able to speak so few words in English, each word he spoke had a lifetime of valuable lessons in it.

One of Grandpa's all-time favorite quotes (especially since he only had a third-grade education) was **"Common sense is not so common."** Then he'd go on to say, "All these book-smart college kids couldn't turn a car key without the label telling them which way to turn it." He'd get so worked up when book-smart people did dumb things. After all the shouting and such, he'd turn to me and say, "You give me ten guys with common sense and we'll outdo a hundred guys with college degrees and no common sense in anything." And his closing sentence was the topper: "But you—you're going to college to make something of yourself."

> ***"The three great essentials to achieve anything worthwhile are: hard work, stick-to-itiveness, and common sense."***
>
> *- Thomas A. Edison*

Imagine the confusion, as a teenager, of thinking college graduates were the enemy, and hard workers without educations built this country—but I was going to college! It took me a few years of living with my grandparents to realize that they were instilling common sense into me, and college was going to be the bonus.

Today, as a consultant to some of the top businesspeople in my industry, I realize that the majority of my coaching direction isn't tied to my degree; it's 90 percent common sense (to me) and 10 percent education.

Once again, thank you, thank you, thank you God, Grandma, Grandpa, Pete, Re-Pete and a fabulous currency exchange. You proved again how simple Grandma and Grandpa wisdom can be profitable.

CHAPTER 8

"Inch by inch life's a cinch; take it by the yard and it gets hard."

ONE OF THE biggest rewards and challenges in my life then and now is going too fast at everything. When I was young, I'd attack my homework so fast, I'd often miss the entire point of the questions asked. Then I'd get a bad grade, and I'd say to the teacher often before thinking about the ramifications, "The way the questions were written was hard to understand and stupidly worded." Wise comments like this often led to me being sent to the principal's office. And, of course, that was often followed by my too rapid response to the principal, which probably sounded like "Who cares? I don't want good grades because I'm not going to be some educated dummy who can't turn a key without a sign telling me to do so!" And Grandpa would demand to know why I was, once again, kicked out of school. Then I would proudly proclaim that he was right, school was stupid, and the smarter people get in school, the dumber they are in life. "I am going to be smart like you, Grandpa." He'd get so mad that he'd stutter, and once again Pete would finish the conversation.

Grandma would say, "Johnny, you have to slow down, think before you talk. Take a moment and think about what is about to come out of your mouth and remember, **Inch by inch, life is a cinch; take it by the yard, and it gets hard.**"

From time to time while putting an "easy to assemble" toy together for my children or a piece of furniture or tool for myself, I'd get so frustrated at how hard the assembly directions were to understand that I'd throw them aside. The outer directions on the box would say to allow forty-five minutes of assembly time. How hard could it be anyway? Then I would attempt to put that item together by looking at the picture on the box. This was supposed to speed up the project but usually led to extra parts that I couldn't find a place for. These extra parts then led to me taking the entire thing apart, setting it aside, slowing down, and actually reading the directions in their entirety. By going step by step, the directions made sense, and I usually completed the forty-five-minute project in only three hours! Trying to speed up the assembly and taking three times, or more, the actual time needed is when I truly started understanding the concept of **"Inch by inch, life is a cinch; take it by the yard, and it gets hard."** Now I often found that by slowing down and going through each part of the directions, I could assemble the item in less than forty-five minutes.

In my early years of business, I once signed a detailed multi-page lease contract without actually understanding what I was signing. I failed to break the lease down to its most important components. I failed to have a business attorney review the lease to protect me and I actually had a contractor build out the entire facility without a building permit. I remember the contractor saying to me this job doesn't require permits because it is not structural. I also remember feeling not so good about his assurance on this permit situation and thinking I should investigate further. Unfortunately, in this case I moved forward without hesitation, to find out on opening day we could not start this business because we had failed to acquire the proper building permits. This rushing without knowing the small details led to a completed buildout, hiring and paying staff for a business that the building inspector made sure would not open for at least twelve more weeks until the plans could be approved. Not knowing the details of this particular lease led to me signing a fifteen-year contract and paying years of rent on a property that this business outgrew in three years. We were certainly thankful that the business grew so fast that we had to move to a bigger location. However, it sure would have been less stressful and more financially rewarding if I had noticed that one little detail, and I would have changed the lease to a three-year lease with multiple three-year options. From that point on, I never signed any documents of importance without our business attorney reading them to me. Inch by inch and piece by piece is a much safer way of getting things done.

"Slow is smooth, and smooth is fast."

- Navy SEAL saying

As I grew older, I made it a game to see how fast I could make excellent decisions, and before I opened my mouth or started an action, I'd quickly process my thoughts and see if I could come up with an even better answer or action—then I would proceed. To get to that level of communication, I'd often wait five to seven seconds before answering any question. This created confusion from time to time with my wife, who thought something was wrong with me not being able to answer simple questions immediately.

Today I still play that game, and it has created amazing results in my businesses, life coaching abilities, and more importantly my amazing marriage and for our children and grandchildren. Try taking life **inch by inch**, and I promise **it will be a cinch**, because I know **if you try to take it by the yard, it gets hard.**

CHAPTER 9

"Obstacles are what we see when we take our eyes off the prize."

I WAS SO blessed to have my grandparents as a teenager, as well as great coaches around me throughout the rest of my life, including today. Those coaches, mentors, and leaders taught me so many great lessons, including the importance of setting goals. Then they directed me in ways to make sure I could often achieve those goals. So many times, I heard, as discussed in Chapter 4, **"What you think about, you talk about, and eventually you bring about."** This little quote taught me to focus my actions and attention on what I wanted to occur and avoid thinking about the obstacles that appeared to be in the way. **"Obstacles are what we see when we take our eyes off the prize"** was another amazing quote that my grandpa and many of my coaches would repeat in several similar forms.

A few weeks after taking the California Chiropractic State Boards in 1985, I received a letter no one wants to receive. This letter stated that my scores on all aspects tested were over 93 percent, except physical therapy, which I received a 74 percent on. A 75 percent or higher was needed in all areas of testing to get my license to practice chiropractic in California. I was initially furious knowing that the physical therapy part of the test was not taught on campus when I was a student. The test was oral, the grading was very subjective, and I was never going to do physical therapy anyway. How could the examiner do this to me? I think at that very moment I felt as if all these years of studying were wasted. I felt like a total failure. I felt so ashamed and compelled to tell my employer, Dr. Pack, that I could not practice in his office until I retook and passed the State Boards and it could easily take six months.

In all my anger and embarrassment, I drove to Dr. Pack's house that evening with the bad news. He could tell right away just by looking at me that something was wrong, and he said, "What great information do you have for me tonight?" Perplexed and thinking that he was going to be upset and fire me on the spot, I told him of my failure and was amazed when he said, "So now that you know and seem to be focused on all that you perceive went wrong, do you think you can focus your attention on the task at hand? The goal is getting your license so I can retire and sell you the practice, isn't it?" As shocked as I was with his reasoning, I could only say, "Yes, sir." For that afternoon I only saw what went wrong (the obstacle) and couldn't see without Dr. Pack's direction that the task at hand (the prize) was what I needed to focus on. Grandpa often would ask me if I was focused on what I couldn't do or on what I could do. He'd follow that question with **"Obstacles are what we see when we take our eyes off the prize."**

Grandma and Grandpa were working-class people and yet they were always more focused on what they could do or give rather than what was wrong or in the way. I remember watching TV with my grandparents and a commercial came on about children being raised in foreign countries without food or water. The spokesperson would say, "For just nineteen dollars per month, you could sponsor a child like this and make all the difference in their world." My grandpa would look at my grandma, and without a word, she would write down the number, call, and make the commitment, and nothing else was said.

Nothing else was said until I opened my mouth and said something like "How do you know they aren't just taking your money?" Grandpa would get so mad that he would stutter, call me over closer to him, and Pete would finish the conversation. Grandpa didn't want to think about the obstacles. He was focused on the positive life changes that he could make for a mere $19.00 per month. In my problem-orientated mind, I could only think, *how do you know your money is getting to that child?* I guess a lot of my skepticism came from the earlier world I lived in that seemed to be all about what we didn't or couldn't ever have, what people could and would steal from me, and not so much about what we could share and what we could give.

When he settled down, Grandpa would try to explain that, if all we do is take and take, there will be nothing left in this world or in our hearts. And if all we do is see the reasons, we cannot accomplish things, we will never accomplish much at all. If we spend most of our time being afraid of doing the wrong thing, we may never do the right thing. However, no matter how much we give to others, we'll always have more to give, and more in our hearts. He'd say, "We make a living by what we get; we make a life by what we give." Later in life, much to my amazement, I found that to be a quote from Winston Churchill, and I can only wonder how Grandpa heard it.

As I studied, experienced, and learned more about life, I realized that a "living" is about "us" and a "life" is about "them." Through consulting today, I realize whenever a client feels like the task, journey, or assignment is just too tough for them, it's almost always because the client makes it all about themselves and is focused on the obstacle more than the goal. The best direction I can give them to free up that confusion is to have the client make everything more about others and keep their eyes on the prize.

"No one has ever become poor by giving."

Anne Frank

When you say, "It's like everyone is taking so many pieces of me, there is nothing left," you can simply change your thought to something like "It's such an honor that so many come to me for advice that it energizes me to help so many by simply staying focused on the prize."

It's true that we make a living by what we get, and we make a life by what we give. If we can train ourselves to only focus on what we want to occur versus what we feel is in the way, we can live a life of knowing that **"obstacles are what we see when we take our eyes off the prize."**

CHAPTER 10

"Cleanliness is next to Godliness."

EVERYONE HAS DIFFERENT views on the concept of cleanliness. In 2016, I was on an expedition above the 64th parallel in the Arctic Circle. Here, for two weeks the temperature never went above -20 degrees. On that adventure I traveled with my friend Ward and three Inuit natives on snow machines. These fine hosts would stop midday and early evening and circle the snow machines to block the constant freezing wind. Then they would place a few caribou pelts on the frozen tundra ground and bring out pieces of hard, frozen caribou or moose meat to cook over a fire, while heating water for coffee or tea. After a few days of this, the buildup on the cooking utensils was quite noticeable to me. Without any available water for cleaning (other than melting snow), I asked one of our guides about the cleanliness of our traveling camp, which led him to share a big frozen smile directed at me as he said, "It is way too cold here for germs to live. You'll be fine." I certainly agreed on the temperature but grossed out by the buildup, I semi-secretly started scraping my utensils and wiping them off.

From that far north adventure to the home of a friend with a modern high-end kitchen with every known cleaning supply, germs can be an issue. After a big beautiful meal, my friend cleaned up the entire kitchen and just prior to an evening night cap as I was about to wash my hands in the kitchen sink, I noticed that this friend failed to rinse out the sink. I asked if it would be okay if I washed down the sink, ran the garbage disposal, and dried it out, only to hear, "Don't worry about it. I like to do that first thing in the morning." This seemed so gross to me. I could only imagine how that sink would smell in the morning and what would be growing in it. Not to mention that "if success loves action," it would make much more sense to finish what he started when he started cleaning the kitchen that evening.

On more than a few occasions in my life, I've thought about the signs in restaurant bathrooms that direct the employees to wash their hands before returning to the kitchen. I can only wonder at what point of deficient hygiene and disease spreading that became a law? I've also left restaurants prior to ordering when the server presented themselves and a quick look at their hands and/or uniform revealed that they hadn't washed either for some time. I can only wonder how many illnesses are transmitted and millions of dollars of business revenue lost because some people don't practice **"cleanliness is next to Godliness."** To most of us a person or business's cleanliness is a direct reflection of that person or business's entire existence. Whether you notice it consciously or subconsciously, it will affect that particular relationship.

Grandma was a meticulous housekeeper in all ways you could possibly imagine. From the floors to the ceilings, as well as from our hearts or minds. Grandpa kept everything in his garage in perfect order and well maintained. A few times, with a light swat of a wooden spoon to the head, Grandma would point out the smallest infraction of the house motto, **"Cleanliness is next to Godliness."**

On Saturdays, which were Grandma's preferred cleaning days, Grandpa would get off work at 7:00 a.m. He and the group of guards he worked with would go play eighteen holes of golf and grab lunch afterward. This five- to six-hour diversion allowed uninterrupted cleaning time for Grandma and me. We'd eat breakfast around 6:00 a.m. and be on our way to cleanliness by 6:30 a.m. Grandma would have us strip the beds first and start the first load of laundry. Then we would wash down the windows, window frames, walls, doors, door handles, light switches, and covers, and then the floorboards, followed by sliding the beds to one side of each room. Then the bed stands were pushed to the side while the floor was being vacuumed.

The moving of the beds often led to the rolling of my eyes and the question, "Grandma, why do we vacuum under the furniture? There is no way dust can get under there." Grandma would laugh and say, **"Cleanliness is next to Godliness."** One time, I remember saying, "Grandma, I don't even think God would notice if we didn't vacuum under the furniture." This of course was immediately followed by the **"Cleanliness is next to Godliness"** quote. This helped create the "God is everywhere and sees everything" mindset I live by today.

Throughout college and grad school, then the next thirty-plus years of my life, there have been hundreds, if not thousands, of times when simply remembering this quote and living this quote created massive opportunities for me.

> *"I will not let anyone walk through my mind with their dirty feet."*
>
> *— Mahatma Gandhi*

The first year of chiropractic school, I lived in a large four-bedroom house on the ground floor, while the owner and her boyfriend lived on the second floor. I believe rent for the downstairs was a whopping $200 per month; so, two of us split that and had plenty of room to study and live without much interference—as long as everything was spotless, and all dishes were immediately washed after use. One day the landlord came downstairs and complimented me on not only being the cleanest tenant she had and always paying my rent two weeks early, but also for the way I always kept the lawn mowed and edged. A few minutes into the conversation, she revealed that she was moving out of the state and wanted me to "manage" the house and rent out all the rooms. I worked out a deal with five other guys to share the entire house as long as it was kept exactly how I wanted it. Each paid $200 per month, creating $1,000 from them. This provided management lessons for me, and the landlord only wanted a total of $400 per month; so, I was generating $600 per month because of the cleanliness rule.

That one little lesson of **"Cleanliness is next to Godliness"** led to six happy college students living in a beautiful, clean house, one incredibly happy landlord receiving her $400 per month rent, and me living in a clean home, rent free throughout college that also paid me an additional $600 per month. **"Cleanliness is next to Godliness"** has paid off very well, for a very long time. I cannot even begin to imagine how many hundreds if not thousands of referrals were and are directed to our clinics because of the simple fact that they are always spotless. My twenty-plus-year building partner and dear friend who runs our land development company has made **"Cleanliness is next to Godliness"** a rule on our job sites. At our build sites everyone stops their projects thirty minutes before the end of their shifts and cleans their portion of the area. This simple action assures that everyone comes to work at a clean job site every morning, without exception. From the bankers and architects, to the surrounding neighbors and businesses, all the way to the laborers, everyone brags about the cleanliness of our sites and I know this has created an environment of people very happy to do business with us. These happy environments create several additional jobs and lots of additional revenues for our companies and all involved.

CHAPTER 11

"It is the simple things in life that matter."

MY OBSERVATION OF truly successful people, and often of their businesses, is that as they grow, they tend to simplify most of their actions. I can tell you with certainty that this simplicity often leads to their lives, relationships, and their businesses growing better, bigger, and stronger than ever before. I remember reading a quote on an Ivory soap wrapper that to this day has made a profound and lasting effect on me. It read, "Enjoy the little things in life, for one day you will look back and realize they were the big things." I read this in 2008, and this little quote has helped me enjoy so much more of what this beautiful life has for me than I ever noticed before.

I encourage you to stop right at this moment and be thankful for at least five things in your life. I realize that you may be thinking of one bad thing in your life that appears to be overwhelming, but please put it aside. Think of five things that you could be thankful for today. Currently, it happens to be freezing outside on our snow-covered ranch in Colorado, and I'm so thankful for our heated home. When was the last time you were openly thankful for the roof over your head? When was the last time you were thankful for your eyes that allow you to see or, in my case, the glasses that allow you to see so much better? We have so much to be thankful for when we focus on the truly important things in our lives. If you are focused on the prize and not the obstacles, you'll often find that **"it is the simple things in life that matter."**

One of the many things my family has been blessed to experience and enjoy is vacationing. Upon examination it wasn't necessarily the vacations themselves that were the highlights as much as the seemingly small moments during those adventures that created the years of enjoyable moments for us. A picture of our youngest son wearing a hula outfit, dancing on the hotel bed at age five, is a moment, and a picture, that will last in our hearts and computers forever. Our daughter boogie boarding and toppling onto the beach at three years old, spitting saltwater and sand out with a look on her face that will bring smiles for years to come. The joy and laughter shared while enjoying a family meal together is ten times more nourishing to our souls than the food being served. My wife and I have the best conversations while going on morning walks, talking about our dreams, our family goals, and often the simple beauty of the morning as the sun greets us. If you change the way you look at things, the things you look at change. We call that *perspective*. **"It is the simple things in life that matter."** Train yourself to be thankful for everything in your life, and soon you will find that the little things are truly the big things.

On Sunday mornings Grandma, Grandpa, and I would head off to church at 9:30 to find a good seat for 10:00 mass. I have no recollection of Pete ever attending Sunday Catholic mass with us. This fact alone created a feeling of freedom that I could sense. After mass, which always seemed to last exactly one hour in our church, we would go to the Italian market and pick up two fresh loaves of bread (which interestingly enough you could smell from the front steps of the church—great marketing), olives, and cheese. When we got home at 11:25, we would passionately eat the fresh, hot bread covered in butter along

45

with the olives and cheese while watching Westerns on the television. Grandma would be laughing and often singing in the kitchen while she drank a little red wine and prepared a magnificent meal to be eaten at noon. This was our Sunday ritual. An amazing thing about this meal was that 90 percent of the time it was spaghetti, sauce, and either pork or chicken. The even more amazing thing about this spectacular meal was that Grandma would make enough to serve it later Sunday night at 6:00, as well as Monday, Tuesday, and often Wednesday nights. To take the amazing even further, it seemed the longer from the initial preparation, the better Grandma's already amazing pasta and sauce tasted.

> *"Sometimes we should express our gratitude for the small and simple things like the scent of the rain, the taste of your favorite food, or the sound of a loved one's voice."*
>
> *- Joseph B. Wirthlin*

Grandpa would tell Grandma and me how these meals were one of the great blessings in our lives. He'd say, **"It is the simple things in life that matter."** Then Grandpa would go on to tell us about the importance of everything from having a loaf of bread to having a roof over our heads. He'd also tell us how blessed we were because he knew that children in Ethiopia never experienced meals like this. And if by any chance you left even a small amount of food on your plate, it was a sin, and that small amount could easily feed an entire family in Ethiopia for months. Once, and only once, I recall asking my grandpa when he had traveled to Ethiopia, and as you can probably imagine, Pete ended that little fact-finding mission of mine right there!

Looking back, I'll bet that Ethiopian story was why Grandma and Grandpa were so charitable with the small amount of money they had. And just as important probably why my wife, our children, and I have focused a portion of our time and resources on helping those who need it. When you get a chance to help out another human being who may not have experienced the same blessings as you, you will truly find out that the small things in life really can be the big things in life. Grandpa was so smart to know and teach the genius of **"It is the simple things in life that matter."**

CHAPTER 12

"Live well—well within your means."

FOR SOME STRANGE and wonderful reason, being raised as a welfare child, I was often attracted to things I was told I would never be able to afford. I remember as a young boy seeing a bright and shiny red Corvette driving down the street, and before the fantasy could even create a smile on my face, someone said to me, "Don't even think about ever having one of those." I remember another time as a kid living in a trailer court in Florida and next to us lived a lady with four boys. I could hardly get over the fact that each of these boys had their own bikes; I used to watch them ride up and down the street as I dreamed of someday riding one of those bikes. Maybe even *owning* one of my own someday. In my future there was a lesson coming out of those boys and one of those bicycles. In a good way as well as a bad way, every time someone told me I couldn't do something, it started a fire that burnt inside me and screamed, "Oh yeah? Just you wait and see."

This imagination along with the fire inside me created a desire to have things, a lot of things. These things early in my life caused two emotions: a desire that led to me almost always figuring out how to obtain these goals, and a false sense of happiness attached to objects. By the time I was thirty-two years old, I had a beautiful showplace of a home in our town and a spectacular weekend home on the water just an hour away. Of course, the main home had high-end furnishings and several luxury cars, and the water home had two expensive boats and several of the newest, high-end Jet Skis. The truth was that I was living way above my means and stressed out of my mind trying to figure out how to pay for all these things. In a short period of time, I realized all the stress in my life was caused by living well—well above my means. I was on the verge of a nervous breakdown from all the stress. I credit the book *Rich Dad, Poor Dad* for changing all that. At that moment I committed to "living well—well within my means."

Within weeks, I had sold the weekend home and paid off most of my debt. I felt so good about that financial decision, I hardly noticed the house was gone. I still had a nice home, but it seemed much nicer when it was paid off. All those material items with their attached debt had created both false happiness and loads of stress. Selling our water home stung psychologically for a short period of time, but the true happiness I was experiencing without the debt was much better than any toy or possession ever was. People would say, "Why in the world did you sell your weekend home? I thought you loved it!" Often, I'd simply reply, "I love my freedom much more." To realize this, I had to find out the hard way that living above my means created much more stress than the false joy of owning things was worth.

Having worked with many business owners over the years, I realized that initially, a lot of my clients who made much more money than my grandparents seemed to never have enough money. Once I started living within my means, I started sharing this rule with my clients: As your income goes up, do not allow your expenses to rise with it. In simple words, **"Live well—well within your means."**

This rule is so simple to follow, and it is just as simple not to follow. Those of us who choose to live well—well within our means—can tell you with certainty that there is nothing as wonderful as your freedom. This freedom doesn't come from things you cannot afford without a bunch of undue stress. I've heard several times that the number one cause of divorce in America has to do with financial issues along with the stress that is carried with them. Imagine the freedom of having little to no debt. Imagine the increased joy and happiness that you would experience every single day without that undue burden. Imagine by following this one simple rule how many more children and adults would never have to experience the long-term pain of divorce.

Thinking back, still to this day, it amazes me how spiritually complete my grandparents were while they lived on such a small amount of money. Grandma had a job working at the local dime store called Ben Franklin's. She worked sixteen to twenty hours per week for minimum wage. The funny thing was she didn't work for the money—she thrived on the interaction with the shoppers. I'll bet the store and the shoppers received much more entertainment from my grandma's loving, warm, and genuinely happy personality than they'll ever know. Grandma loved talking about how much fun she had at the store.

Grandpa was employed at a factory, working a third shift guard job, and probably didn't make much more per hour in his full-time position. That being said, there was always food on the table, clean clothes to wear, and a roof over our head. And the roof over our head was paid for long before I showed up.

> *"Annual income twenty pounds, annual expenditure nineteen six, result happiness. Annual income twenty pounds, annual expenditure twenty-pound ought and six, result misery."*
>
> *— Charles Dickens*

Grandpa was often heard saying that you borrow money two times in your life: once for your first house and second for your first business. He was quick to finish that statement with "I only borrowed money once because I never started a business, and I paid off that one mortgage loan in less than seven years!"

I heard that brilliant lesson over and over, yet still had to find that one lesson out for myself as an adult. I sure wish Pete could have jumped in when Grandpa was giving that lesson to pound it into my thick head! This turned out to be an example of me knowing but not doing. At thirty-two years of age, I knew this lesson but found myself with a big mortgage on our main home and another big mortgage on our water home, as well as two vehicle payments and a few credit cards that never seemed to be paid off. The stress of so much money going out every month was mentally and physically debilitating. That ongoing pressure almost pushed me over the edge until one day I found myself quoting Grandpa to two of my favorite young patients: **"Live well—well within your means.** Never get stuck on the wrong side of interest, and only borrow money two times in your life: your first home and your first business." Somehow by quoting Grandpa's brilliance, it ignited his words in my heart and head. I took immediate action and made plans to pay off everything; if I couldn't pay it off in a short period of time, I'd sell it. And the pressure associated with it was gone too.

I'd also like to send many, many thanks here to Robert T. Kiyosaki, who wrote *Rich Dad, Poor Dad*. I remember buying his amazing book on a Friday, reading it after dinner that evening, and finishing it in about eighteen straight hours. Then I prepared a plan which included selling our prized water home and being on the good side of interest from then on. God bless you, Grandpa and Robert T. Kiyosaki, on anchoring the brilliance of **"Live well—well within your means."** Oh, if only Pete would have shown up earlier for this gem. Once again, it's the days that break you that make you—if you're willing to do what you know you should do.

CHAPTER 13

"God is always watching."

WHEN TRAINING MY children, grandchildren, and even new employees, I often bring up my belief that our Creator is always watching us. If you look in the Bible, you can find a dozen verses that explain this. One verse that comes to mind is from Proverbs 15:3: "The eyes of the Lord are everywhere, keeping watch on the wicked and the good." To add impact to that image for non-religious people, I have them imagine they're being followed by a film crew and three of their closest friends. Imagine how you would handle any and every situation if that were your audience! Hopefully we always do good, especially when no one is watching. However, if we need extra incentive, this image has really helped me and non-believers alike, and I believe it could do the same for you.

If you are even slightly challenged by the idea that our Creator is omnipresent, then the image of a film crew and three close friends will be helpful for you. I once was consulting a business owner who was conflicted between settling for delivering an average product versus working to deliver a really good product. If he lived by these Grandma and Grandpa rules, he could have thought, as stated in Chapter 2, **"Anything worth doing is worth doing well"** or, as in Chapter 3, **"Do unto others as you would want them to do unto you,"** or even

Chapter 6, **"Reputation, reputation, reputation—that's all you've got."** All three of these rules together would have given him the same answer I did. He chose to deliver the really good product, and the rest of this business story was lined in gold.

This is a simple example of living by a set of rules and doing the right thing *because* it is the right thing. In the minds of those who make decisions without clear rules I can see confusion and lack of clarity. Some believe their decisions are complicated by cost and profitability, but I believe an even better decision could be made every time, without exception, by simply using the above three rules.

I believe we have a problem when doctors give patients care plans based on that patient's insurance coverage, lack of coverage, or their perceived financial situation versus what would be prescribed if that patient happened to be their mother. I believe we have a problem when product designers create products that save companies a few pennies initially but eventually end up not only harming the user but costing the company much of their profit as well. I believe pharmaceutical companies would create safer products or admit they can't if the user was their mother and they weren't simply driven by the almighty dollar. I'm going to climb off my soapbox now, but remember, **"God is always watching."** I suggest you look at how much better, safer, and more profitable living by these rules could make you.

When Grandma wanted me to learn something, she had this amazing, subtle way of anchoring her message deep inside my head that to this day still amazes me. Her words could leave a feeling inside me that is hard to explain, but I know I never wanted to let her down. Grandpa had an entirely different way of pounding lessons into my hard head. Lord knows how much I needed all of their techniques.

"You can never go where God is not."

- Max Lucado

I vividly remember a day when I was playing catch out in front of my grandparents' home with a friend, and my errant throw went over my friend's head and through the living room picture window. My friend ran all the way to his house without ever looking back. In the coming hours before my grandparents returned, I thought of a thousand excuses to use when Grandma and Grandpa got home that would hopefully result without Pete. Then they pulled into the driveway, and Grandpa got out of his Chevrolet Impala screaming at the top of his lungs for me. Scared to death, knowing all my rehearsed excuses would not make a difference, I appeared with my baseball glove still on. Grandpa stuttered and eventually asked, "What in the holy hell happened to the living room picture window?" With the glove still on, I said, "I have no idea." And as he looked through the broken glass and saw a baseball, surrounded by glass, lying in the center of the living room, I swear my heart stopped. Thank goodness Grandpa and Pete knew good old-fashioned CPR and my heart was restarted instantly. I think without going into too much detail you understand how much I needed that lesson: There is never a good time to lie because **"God is always watching."**

After Grandpa finished sharing his input with me and I was told about a dozen times what a pain in the butt I was, all I could think of was why in the heck I didn't hide the ball and glove. Obviously, this is not the thought I would have had if I knew at that time my Creator was watching. If I simply lived by a rule of doing what is right, especially when no one is watching, I would have had a much better action than thinking about hiding the evidence. The real lesson came about an hour later—when I had finally stopped making excuses and fessed up to my mistake—and Grandma came into my room and said, **"God is always watching."** Those words to this day are in my every thought and action in all I think, say, or do.

CHAPTER 14

"Fifteen minutes early is on time, on time is late, and it is NEVER okay to be late."

I AM LUCKY to be married to my incredible wife, and one of the many reasons is because she is aware of time. Time awareness has always been important to her and to me. We're the kind of people who arrive at the airport three hours early (or more) just in case. We're both early to everything we do. In fact, if you invite us to dinner at six, you can count on us arriving before that because we always allow for extra time. We never have to rush, we never have to speed, we always get good parking and even better seats, and we never have to be stressed out or in a hurry.

Two of my golden rules as an employer were that attendance is mandatory and your pay is determined by your performance. During our hiring process we would initially hold group interviews of the top dozen candidates for a particular position. We would often hold these group interviews at 6:45 p.m., which would allow the candidates and ourselves plenty of time to complete our workdays. In these evening interviews we could always count on two things: the sharpest potential employees would arrive between 6:15 and 6:30, and someone would arrive after 6:45. We would lock the front doors at exactly 6:45, and the late arrivals would knock and knock until one of us opened the door. Without exception we would open the door just enough to see a frazzled person with an excuse as to why they were late. We'd never let them in and as politely as possible say that being late to an interview is a very good indication of their future punctuality.

A good friend of mine says, "Success leaves clues." I can add to that by saying, "Failure leaves clues." We had another little rule that if any employee was late, even by a minute, in the first ninety days, we'd let them go that day. You might say that is way too strict, but I would say that our top five employees were with us between ten and fifteen years when I sold our last business, and none of us were ever late to work. In fact, we all prided ourselves on being fifteen minutes or more early so we could be completely ready when the doors opened. Lucky for me and my businesses, the Grandma and Grandpa rule of **"fifteen minutes early is on time, on time is late, and it is NEVER okay to be late"** was taught by more than just my grandparents.

In my thirty years of active chiropractic practice taking care of hundreds of amazing families and thousands of individuals, two things I'd often bring up with patients and potential employees were: 1) In all that time the latest I ever arrived to work was thirty-two minutes early and 2) I missed four days of work in that entire time—three days after a knee surgery and one day when my back was so bad I couldn't get out of bed. My grandparents taught me that attendance is mandatory, and the benefits of life came from your excellent performance. When I'd share that with patients or potential employees, I could tell right away very few people were raised with the idea that **"fifteen minutes early is on time, on time is late, and it is NEVER okay to be late."**

Grandma and Grandpa were obsessed with the idea of one's word meaning everything. After all, honoring your word is what creates your reputation, and you would never tarnish your reputation on purpose, especially with something as simple as being on time.

One day I asked Grandpa why being early was so important to him, and as the words came out of my mouth, I remember hoping Pete wouldn't jump in to explain. Understand that I never believed Grandpa to be abusive even with the use of Pete. I was extremely hard-headed, and Pete was just one of the blessings he bestowed on me—a blessing that truly positively changed the direction of my entire being. Thankfully Grandpa went on to explain that a man is only as good as his word and that everything, no matter how small, mattered and everything counted because everything affected everything. This thought directed every action I took from that moment on until today. Everything mattered, everything counted, and everything affected everything; it was a way of being incredibly responsible for every thought or action I ever took. Grandpa believed that if a man would lie about something as small as time, he'd lie about anything.

"Living with integrity means: Not settling for less than what you know you deserve in your relationships. Asking for what you want and need from others. Speaking your truth, even though it might create conflict or tension. Behaving in ways that are in harmony with your personal values. Making choices based on what you believe, and not what others believe."

- Barbara De Angelis

What about things you cannot control, like an accident or a flat tire? Ultimately you cannot control those sorts of things, but you *can* control how you respond to them. What I believe Grandpa meant by that is if you always drove on good tires and left early enough to change a flat tire, should you have one, you could still be early to your destination. Certainly, an accident would require more time than anyone could plan for, but Grandpa would go on to tell you that the reason people get in accidents is often because they left late and were driving too fast.

It was such a blessing for me to have this time awareness instilled into me at this formative time in my life. Leaving plenty early has benefitted my children, my incredible wife, and me in a multitude of ways over the years. We try not to brag on our children and often leave that up to others, but I will say that several times coaches, other parents, employers, and teachers have positively commented on our children's punctuality. My wife can take leaving early to an entirely different level. Sometimes I think her time management rule would be "If you are not at least an hour early, you are late!" That being said, it is amazing to be in a family with people who value time awareness this way.

CHAPTER 15

"What doesn't kill us makes us stronger."

AT THIS STAGE of our time together, I completely understand that this chapter's title and my grandpa's occasional use of Pete may ruffle the feathers of some modern-day thinkers. I can assure you that this was an incredibly valuable lesson in forming the person I am today and quite probably so many other successful people. I also firmly believe that if everyone had the opportunity to read this book, there would never be a time where Pete (backhands or spankings) would be necessary. Discipline can come in many different forms when raising children, but please don't give your children everything you never had and be so perplexed when they turn out like the kids you never liked. Without the structure of rules, our society would not fare well. At any point in my teen years, while living with my phenomenal grandparents, when I wanted to give up on anything, I was reminded that once you make a habit of quitting, you will create a quitter in yourself forever. Looking back, on a more positive note, I wonder why the lesson wasn't worded as *if you never give up and always move positively forward, you will create a winner in yourself forever.*

Grandma would often notice me daydreaming when I was supposed to be doing something like my homework. She would say, "Don't ever quit until you're done, but if your project is daydreaming, you're doing just fine." The pain of disappointing her was much greater than anything Grandpa or Pete ever "told" me. My grandma and several teachers used to call me "Jon the Daydreamer." Oftentimes I'd be somewhere and then in an instant be somewhere else—in my mind. Later in my life I turned this activity into goal setting and achieving. I'm convinced this was a direct reflection of the combination of my grandparents' influence.

> *"Strength does not come from winning. Your struggles develop your strengths. When you go through hardships and decide not to surrender, that is strength."*
>
> *- Arnold Schwarzenegger*

Grandpa and Pete were a little more direct with their approach to this subject. For example, one day I got caught daydreaming in a freshman class and was directed to the principal's office for disrespectful behavior. I instantly felt at that point that the humiliation of that occurring in front of my classmates was more than enough punishment. Apparently, I was the only one feeling no more punishment was due. On my walk of shame, I slowly made my way to the office. After waiting and fearing for the worst for over fifteen minutes, I was directed into the principal's office to state my case. He turned out to be easy to talk to and much more like my grandma than my grandpa. He said my daydreaming was creative and very good for me but would have to be done at the right times and in the proper places. He went on to explain that someday when I was old enough to drive, my daydreaming could cause an accident and kill someone. I was directed to write "I will not daydream in any class ever again" 500 times and to have one of my grandparents sign that paper before I turned it back into him the next day. He further stated that **"what doesn't kill us makes us stronger."**

I quickly finished the 500 sentences before the school day was over and thought for hours on how "Jon the Daydreamer" could get Grandma to sign without Grandpa's involvement. Grandpa worked the 11:00 p.m. to 7:00 a.m. shift as a guard and usually was deep asleep when I got home from school, so I immediately went for it. That well-thought-out plan of mine came to a screeching stop when out of the blue, Grandpa woke up and noticed the sentences on his way to the refrigerator. Without much fanfare he went into a tirade about how embarrassing that was for our family, and before I could even agree or apologize, Pete jumped into the action…and you know the rest.

On a lighter note, still to this day I'm convinced that my grand-pa, with the collusion of Pete, invented the concept of a "timeout." Nowadays a "timeout" means standing in a corner, but for me it meant a whack on the head. Please, before you freak out, I truly doubt that I was ever knocked unconscious. I probably exaggerate this a bit, but after Pete's action I'd ask what happened and Grandpa would say, "You had a little timeout." Grandma would jump in and tell Grandpa that everything I did didn't require a backhand, only to hear him proclaim, **"What doesn't kill you makes you stronger,"** and a simple backhand never killed anyone. Oh, how different that timeout is from standing in a corner today for our children's timeout. A very wise person and mentor, Dr. Wayne Pack, once told me that people give their children everything they never had (except discipline) only to find them turning out like the people they never appreciated. Then the parents will spend the rest of their lives wondering what they did wrong. He also told me that if we properly raise our children, we will get a chance to spoil our grandchildren, but if we spoil our children, we'll end up raising our grandchildren.

CHAPTER 16

"If it sounds too good to be true, it probably is."

THREE MONTHS AFTER graduating from chiropractic college, I landed a fantastic associateship with Dr. Wayne Pack. Dr. Pack was sixty-five years old and I was twenty-five. He had an excellent reputation in our community, over thirty years of practice experience, and I wanted to learn all he knew. **"Reputation, reputation, and reputation—that's all you've got!"** popped into my thoughts. I was working Monday through Saturday and going in on Sunday to clean the office for a few extra dollars. This was the required effort Dr. Pack told me it took to build a practice. I was up for anything he'd throw my way. During one of our daily talks about life, patient care, and practice, I mentioned to him that starting a practice took more effort and many more working hours than I anticipated. He smiled and said, "I don't think it will kill you." I could only smile inside, knowing full well Grandpa might have added, **"What doesn't kill you makes you stronger."** Within a few months of being in my new town, I had an encounter with an older wise gentleman that locked in another Grandma and Grandpa rule.

At that time in my life, I was just leaving the office and driving my trusty 1970 Volkswagen pop top camper bus, which was most certainly on its last leg. I hadn't let Dr. Pack, or anyone know that I had a Mercedes 420 SEL and a Porsche 928 paid for with free and clear US titles, stored and preparing for sale. In 1985, the sale of these two vehicles I imported from Germany during college would allow me to buy my first home. There I was at a gas station, filling up my bus, when this older stranger approached me. Being that I just left the office, I was in a suit and tie, and he smiled and complimented me on my suit. He then commented on memories he had of the days when he owned a VW bus. Once he captured my attention, he went on to tell me it would be much easier to build a practice driving a vehicle that more positively represented my status as an "up and coming" young doctor in my community. I remember saying, "Yes, someday I would love to drive a Mercedes or even a Porsche." He said, "Those vehicles would scream, 'I'm a big shot and a showoff,' and you'd instantly create the wrong reputation in our community." Now he really had my attention, so I asked him what type of vehicle should an up and coming young doctor such as myself drive. Without any hesitation he said a four-door Buick or Chevrolet would be perfect until I had enough time in practice to afford a Cadillac. This man obviously held a wealth of information, and I felt compelled to find out more about him.

Two days after this gas station event, this older, wise gentleman and I went to lunch. During the lunch, I was explaining that I was just starting practice and in no way could afford a newer vehicle. He paused and told me that I should at least clean up and paint my bus. Within a few minutes after that sentence was delivered, he called a friend who happened to own an automotive paint shop. A few minutes later there was a driver out in front of the restaurant who drove away with my bus. I didn't have the cash to pay for the paint job immediately, so he convinced me that if he held the title until I paid for it, he would cover me. This once-in-a-lifetime encounter at a gas station led me to becoming friends with this older, wiser man who was willing to help me in so many ways! I thought this was exactly how everything was supposed to work out.

As I walked back to the office with a huge smile on my face, it had not sunk in that I left that lunch meeting not only paying the entire lunch bill, but also without my VW bus or its title. I was so excited to tell the entire story to Dr. Pack that I barely listened when he said, "It sounds way too good to be true, don't you think?" Then it hit me like a ton of bricks. **"If it sounds too good to be true, it probably is."** To make a long story short, it took me months to straighten out this lesson, and by the time I did get my bus back, I had to pay the paint shop much more than a normal paint job would cost at the time, some court dues, and a duplicate title fee. I did not realize it then but did eventually come to understand that those expenses were well worth the lesson I had learned. After that experience, I trained myself to perform my due diligence, and then if anyone or anything still felt too good to be true, I'd run away.

Even earlier in my life as a teenager, I was obsessed with cars and motorcycles. As a result, I seldom ever saved my hard-earned dollars for very long. I definitely owned some cool cars though. During my junior year of high school, I remember coming home to share some amazing news with my grandparents about a once-in-a-lifetime deal I stumbled into. Through the grapevine, I heard of a 1966 427-cubic-inch marine-blue Corvette convertible in almost excellent shape that could be purchased for ONLY $4,200 and was going to be scooped up quickly by some very lucky person if I didn't buy it today. Before I could even finish my sales pitch, without even looking up at me, Grandpa said, **"If it sounds too good to be true, it probably is."**

> *"One who listens learns; one who learns listens; one who listens and learns is on the path to enlightenment."*
>
> *- Matshona Dhliwayo*

I was so sure that Grandpa had no idea what he was talking about that I smiled and went straight to the bank and withdrew 99 percent of my savings to come up with the $4,200. I knew once my grandpa saw this amazing deal, he'd probably want to go into business with me buying and selling vehicles and making millions! Within an hour, I was pretty much the coolest guy on the road driving this one-in-a-million find. As I got closer and closer to my grandparents' home, the temperature gauge rose higher and higher until just as I pulled into the driveway, the engine blew up. Grandma and Grandpa came outside just in time to witness steam blowing out from every opening around the engine compartment and oil pouring onto the driveway. This must have really stirred up the pot of emotions for both of my grandparents because I swear, they both said in unison, **"If it sounds too good to be true, it probably is."**

By the time I'd paid for the engine to be rebuilt, which upon further observation led to the transmission and rear end both having to be rebuilt as well, and of course paying to have my grandparents' driveway re-slurry coated because of the oil spill, I was absolutely flabbergasted to end up putting $9,000 into my, at the time, $4,200 car. I'm absolutely sure that this expensive lesson saved me hundreds of thousands of dollars, if not more, throughout my life. Who knows, but if Pete would've jumped in on this lesson, maybe millions of dollars could have been saved during my lifetime.

CHAPTER 17

"Money can't buy you happiness."

GROWING UP WITHOUT the luxury of a father or father figure in my life made me more concerned about simply getting by rather than the thought of thriving. Don't get me wrong, getting by can be a very powerful motivator, which it was for me. One painful but sometimes wonderful part of that motivation for me was the need to have nice things. Fancy items like bicycles, motorcycles, cars, and other toys seemed to make me feel better about myself or at least that is what I thought at the time. Somehow early in my life, I started associating not having these nice things as bad. That bad feeling created a burning desire in me to obtain these sports cars and luxury items. Somehow, I would create a way to obtain those luxuries, and I would feel good for a short period of time, until I realized that there was something else out there that I didn't have. This realization caused me to feel more dark emotions, which created that burning desire to feel a sense of accomplishment, and the cycle repeated itself over and over again. Eventually the ups and downs of this sort of life of having or not having became spiritually exhausting.

Even after years of appearing successful to the world around me, I came to the conclusion that the possessions were not what made me happy. At that time, I decided it was the pursuit of those "dreams" that created happiness inside me. With this newfound wisdom, I noticed that there were less emotional ups and downs for me, yet there was still confusion. From then on, when I started to achieve, instead of keeping the money, I would donate it. This new way of life was, and still is today, very gratifying. I enjoyed the thrill of pursuing an achievement but savored the added bonus of giving that achievement away.

For my fiftieth birthday twelve of my coaching clients got together and bought me a bright red Ferrari. They surprised me with this fabulous gift at a seminar I put on in San Francisco that year. I was truly speechless as well as overwhelmed that they thought that much of me and our working relationship. In the months to come, I noticed an amazing amount of fun (most likely ego gratification) in telling people that my clients bought a Ferrari for me as a birthday present. And my clients realized there was a great deal of pride and satisfaction in telling others that they had bought their friend a Ferrari.

After a few years of owning that masterpiece car, I realized that I had driven it less than one thousand miles and I had told the story so many times, it wasn't working its magic on me anymore. I donated the car to a charity that helped veterans and once again felt fabulous…for a while. Then I realized I was once again back on an emotional roller coaster of up and down, win or lose, and I knew that wasn't the way life was supposed to be.

One day while observing my incredible wife laughing her heart out while in the kitchen talking with our two younger children, I asked, "How is it you are always so happy?" In less than a microsecond she smiled and said, "Happiness is a choice, and I choose to be happy!" I thought, *It cannot possibly be that easy—can it?* If chasing accomplishments was not creating long-term happiness and obtaining things and giving them away wasn't the answer either, maybe my wife was right. I asked her about our magnificent home and vacations, which she said were fantastic but that is not where happiness comes from. Those things are a blessing that I am very thankful for, but you must know that **"money can't buy you happiness."** We talked about this choice of being happy for months until we both decided that she should write a book so that the world could be blessed with what the happiest person I know knows about happiness. A short time later, her book, _HAPPYness Is HERE,_ written by Danyel Baker & created by YOU, was published. We both believe the world we live in can be not only an awesome adventure, but more fun, more profitable, and certainly much happier as long as we live by a simple set of rules. Grandma and Grandpa's rules along with my wife's rule of choosing happiness are a great start.

One of the top five amazing lessons that were taught to me by Grandma and Grandpa that has helped me with my family and so many other people throughout the years is Grandpa's philosophy on money. Whether I was sharing his philosophy with employees, family, or patients, this is certainly the one lesson that the people thank me for the most often. Acting on this lesson alone could change your financial situations in the most amazing ways; however, make sure to utilize _all_ of the wisdom my grandparents shared with me. I believe that each little piece of what I call their "Wisdom to create an Amazingly Healthy & Wealthy Life with Love from Grandma & Grandpa" is so much more powerful when combined.

> _"It is not the man who has too little, but the man who cannot be happy because he craves so much more that is poor."_
>
> _- Seneca_

I'll bet that Grandpa and Grandma's combined income never went past $30,000 in any given year and was possibly far less. Yet, they owned their car and home without loans and they never lacked for anything that I knew of. Oftentimes while living with my grandparents, I was saving and just as quickly spending my money. Grandpa would say, "If all you care about is money, just know that **money can't buy you happiness.**"

Grandpa's golden rule for money was so easy that I believe it was often just as easy to forget. Embarrassing as it is to share, I broke this rule several times early in my adulthood, which caused several hard times in my family's life. It's so simple to do that it was just as simple not to do. Here it is, as Grandpa would say: "You borrow money twice in your life—once for your first business and once for your first home, and that's it. You then pay those off and never borrow money again. You live well—well within your means." Apparently, this rule was for my entrepreneurial spirit because Grandpa only borrowed money once, which was to purchase his home.

CHAPTER 18

"Worrying is like rocking in a rocking chair. It will give you something to do, but it will never take you anywhere."

AS A TEENAGER, I had a very creative and imaginative mind that could easily drift off into a daydream. I also had the terrible habit of always imagining the worst outcome that could possibly happen in any situation. For example, while taking a test at school, I'd imagine that I failed it, which led to it probably happening because I wasn't focused in the first place and probably was daydreaming during the test. That would lead to me imagining being kicked out of school and removed from my grandparents' home, which of course left me thinking that I had somehow embarrassed and shamed my grandparents. Then there was Pete to deal with and so on. I'd come home and my grandma would say, "Jonny, what are you so worried about now?" I'd tell her the entire conjured up story that I had fabricated in my mind, and she would look at me with that unconditionally loving face and say, **"Worrying is like rocking in a rocking chair. It will give you something to do, but it will never take you anywhere."** I would love to tell you that her simple statement ended my nightmare of mental creations, but this one took more time.

> *"Keep your face to the sunshine and*
> *you cannot see a shadow."*
>
> *- Helen Keller*

As a teenager I'd be at one of my jobs, and if even for a brief moment I thought I could have given a customer better service than what they had already received, I'd instantly imagine getting fired and embarrassing my grandparents, only to be removed from their amazing loving environment and placed somewhere terrible. This in a millisecond would lead to me doing something even worse in my mind, and next thing you know I pictured myself in prison. I would share these thoughts with Grandma and sometimes she would laugh or sometimes her eyes would well up with tears, but no matter what, she'd say, **"Worrying is like rocking in a rocking chair. It will give you something to do, but it will never take you anywhere."** And during one of these golden moments, I finally started asking positive questions that would set me free for a lifetime of positive mental creativity.

I asked, "Grandma, how can I go somewhere positive with these terribly scary thoughts always in my mind?" Again, her beautiful, loving energy had the perfect answer. "Jonny, if you can imagine the worst, simply know that you can turn that around and imagine the best. You must take your daydreaming and worst thoughts and turn them into positive daydreaming and positive thoughts." From that moment on when I'd drift off into a negative daydream, I'd direct that thought into something amazing. For example, if the instant thought was a car wreck, I'd turn that into a bright and shiny new car, often a bright red Corvette, with plenty of people looking at me and thinking, *What a lucky guy.*

Years ago, I made it my goal to work one day per week. As a business consultant I chose to work a quick sixteen-hour day on Tuesdays. I schedule thirty-two twenty-minute calls on that day to stay connected to the offices and businesses I consult. Incidentally, I am always available to my clients. If they need anything, they simply call my cell phone, but for the most part, one twenty-minute call per month keeps us on track. My group of amazing business owners, on any given Tuesday, have small clinics that collect anywhere from $500,000 to $3,000,000 per year depending on location. All of these offices are top performers in their professions. One very clear pattern I have observed over the last thirty-plus years of working with these amazing businesses is the fact that the offices that collect, say, $1,000,000 or less per year are run by people who have very vivid imaginations about what could go **wrong** when a new concept or procedure is introduced. Conversely, the businesses or offices that collect well over a million dollars per year are run by people who have very vivid imaginations about what could go **right** when shown a new concept or procedure.

> An example of a server who tends to worry negatively when introduced to a new procedure might go something like this: They are told by their manager that when approaching a table for the first time, they must have a warm, genuine smile and concern for those customers' overall dining experience. This will instantly create better rapport, and they will enjoy the entire experience, leading them to most likely spend more. The worrier instantly thinks about what would happen if they're not nice enough.

An example of a business owner who tends to worry negatively when introduced to a new procedure might be something like this. They are told that if they manage their people like they would like to be managed themselves, their production will go up. The worrier instantly says, "There is no way you will get much work out of people who are not constantly pushed."

An example of a doctor who tends to worry negatively when introduced to a new procedure might be something like this. They are told that during a consultation with a patient, they must completely understand the patient's point of view to truly serve that patient. And a big part of that understanding comes from allowing that patient to feel safe enough in the consultation to tell them more than superficial information. And they must go into more detail when taking a consultation to truly serve their patient's needs and find out what is wrong. The doctor's instant worried thought is "Well, in my office we are already an hour behind every day, and that procedure would put us much further behind."

I have observed over the last thirty-plus years of working with these amazing businesses that the offices that collect $1,000,000 or more per year are run by people who have very vivid imaginations about what could go **right**. If you must think something, think something positive, because worrying is not going to move you forward no matter what you do for a living.

As a constant reminder to myself and as a consultant to some very successful people, a big part of my job is often helping them redirect their not so great "what ifs" into amazingly positive "what ifs." Several times per day I say to myself and others, **"Worrying is like rocking in a rocking chair. It will give you something to do, but it will never take you anywhere."**

CHAPTER 19

"Good fences make good neighbors."

MY AMAZING GRANDMA loved and appreciated just about everyone and everything. Grandpa was a bit more protective of his space. Sometimes when Grandpa was being a bit too protective, Grandma would say, "Andy, could you please be a little friendlier?" Grandpa would look at her and often not say a word; his face said it all. But when he would respond to that question, it often sounded like this: **"Good fences make good neighbors."** Grandpa was talking in general about keeping a distance between himself and others more than simply talking about his specific neighbors. He'd go on to declare that if you let people get too close to you and something goes wrong, you will wish that you weren't so close to them.

"Don't be dismayed at goodbyes. A farewell is necessary before you can meet again. And meeting again, after moments or lifetimes, is certain for those who are friends."

- Richard Bach

A great example of this was the six-foot lilac bush wall between my grandparents' home and the neighbors. You may remember from an earlier chapter when I temporarily messed up that little bit of Grandpa's safety. It wasn't as if Grandpa was ever rude to people; it was just that he wasn't overly inviting to them. Grandma would want to invite the neighbors over for food, and Grandpa would have none of that, protesting, **"Good fences make good neighbors."** He would explain that if they got close with the neighbors and even a minor issue occurred between the two, they'd live the rest of their lives with that dispute keeping them apart in one way or another. For the rest of their lives, they would dread coming home or going outside, in fear that they would run into the neighbors and have to pretend that they were happy with each other. Grandpa believed blood was thicker than water, and all issues could be worked out within families, but everyone else was different.

Always the one trying to bring my two cents into the situation, I looked in the Bible to find the verse about loving thy neighbor. This discovery led me to think that Grandpa would be impressed that not only did I go to church with them, but I also read and took interest in the Bible. I found in Matthew 22:36-40, *(36) Jesus said unto him, thou shalt **love** the Lord God with all **thy** heart, and with all **thy** soul, and with all **thy** mind. (38) This is the first and great commandment. (39) And the second **is** like unto it. Thou shalt **love thy neighbor** as thyself. (40) On these two commandments hang all the prophets.* I was convinced upon finding this biblical wisdom that I could certainly help Grandpa with his rule. The key would be in the timing of the presentation. Then it happened when we were coming home from church. The neighbors were out in their front yard upon our arrival. As always Grandpa got out of the car and opened Grandma's door. Grandpa also believed that it was the duty of the man to open a lady's door. As Grandma got out of the car, I heard her say, "Let's go say hello and invite them for pasta." Without hesitation Grandpa said, "We'll go over and say hello, and then we'll go home and eat lunch. Remember, **good fences make good neighbors."** We abided by Grandpa's direction. We went over, said hello, and then went home to eat lunch, without guests. I knew that today would be my opening to enlighten Grandpa on the second commandment.

We opened the front door with our fresh baked Italian bread and olives in hand as we were greeted by the heavenly aroma of my grandma's spaghetti sauce. I knew that the sauce had been simmering since before the sun came up because that was one of Grandmas Sunday ritual. Even today the smell of spaghetti sauce cooking is one of the few things in the world that bring back great memories for me. Fresh baked bread and spaghetti sauce simmering on the stove is such a heavenly memory. As I changed out of my Sunday church clothes, I prepared for the biblical lesson I was about to share with my grandparents. During that amazing meal, I found two really good opportunities in the conversation to interject my newfound knowledge but chickened out both times. Then after the meal while sitting in the living room watching a Western movie, during a commercial I casually said to my grandpa, "How is it that in the Bible, the second commandment says, *Thou shalt love thy neighbor as thyself* and you always tell us **'Good fences make good neighbors.'"** Grandpa looked at me as if he was proud of my research and thought process only to proclaim that to truly love and respect your neighbor you would always be available to help them, and you would always keep some distance from them. End of conversation.

In business and in life, I have to admit that no matter how many times I tested Grandpa's rule, he was always correct. This rule about neighbors always made business dealings better to not get over friendly. You should always be respectful and friendly, but once you get too close, you open the door for simple business statements like "No thank you, I'm not interested" to create feelings of rejection.

This rule has helped me create many long-lasting, mutually beneficial working relationships throughout my life with patients, staff, and clients. It seemed that until I acted on Grandpa's wisdom, I would make friends with patients and something trivial would come up and soon I didn't have that friend and wasn't caring for that particular patient anymore. I would befriend a staff member and soon something I thought trivial would occur and shortly after I didn't have that friend or that staff member.

During the middle of 2008, after the big economic housing crash, our land development company, in which I am a 50 percent partner, was working hard to keep our construction crews off welfare. My role in this company is mainly the financial part. My partner, Mike, has been in the land development and building industry for over forty years. He knows more in a minute about this subject than I will know in my lifetime, so I usually stay out of his way when building. However, I know that **"if you're going to expect anything from anyone, you must inspect everything from everyone."** So, one day I decided to look into the bids on a certain project a bit deeper than my usual acceptance of Mike's knowledge, and I noticed a cement bill for $160,000, which seemed a bit expensive. Before I asked Mike about this amount, I called the owner of the cement company and questioned him about the amount. Long story short, in about three minutes he agreed the bid was a bit high and lowered it to $126,500. That was an instant $33,500 savings from one of the many contractors on this project. I thought that was a pretty big oversight on Mike's part and could only wonder what else we were being overcharged for. After calming down a bit I called for a meeting with Mike and the cement company owner. During the meeting it was instantly apparent that Mike and the cement company owner had been close friends for so long that Mike stopped examining his bids and simply accepted them as presented. Mike went on to say that questioning a close friend's bid seemed rude. My instant response was "That is exactly why my grandpa always said, '**Good fences make good neighbors.'**" The three of us decided at that meeting friendships were too costly if we couldn't afford them. In that one case Grandpa's rule saved my company a lot of money. I went on to oversee all bids from that point on. It was always my policy to be friendly and respectful with all the contractors and related businesspeople I dealt with. I actually would say that being friendly and respectful toward all people was my policy. In business I kept just enough distance from others that it was clear our business was always business.

CHAPTER 20

"They will never care how much you know until they know how much you care."

WHILE AT THE Palmer School of Chiropractic in Davenport, Iowa, I was amazed at how smart I thought I was becoming and how my friends back home were not. I'd come home and show off my big developing fancy doctor vocabulary and wonder why my friends didn't know what I was saying. I'll bet I didn't even know what I was saying. I'd be gone at school for months at a time, studying like crazy, learning big fancy words, and passionately convincing myself I could actually someday not only use those words in conversation but also get my doctorate degree. The power of our thoughts is mind-boggling. Incidentally, every time I wanted to quit graduate school (and there were many times it seemed too tough for me), I'd remember "the look" and that promise to God, Grandpa, and my chiropractor; so I'd pull it together and progress forward with my studies.

"Promises are the uniquely human way of ordering the future, making it predictable and reliable to the extent that this is humanly possible."

- Hannah Arendt

When home, I'd complain about everything to my grandparents from how tough school was, how dumb I must be, and how dumb my friends were getting. Grandma would say with so much love that I wasn't dumb, nor were my friends getting dumber; I was simply getting smarter. Then in the same breath, she reminded me not to get too big for my britches. Grandpa would jump in and say things like, "If you get so smart you can't talk to people, what kind of doctor do you think you'll become?" Then he'd tell me about my patients by saying, **"They will never care how much you know until they know how much you care."** At that time in my life I was six inches taller than my grandpa and outweighed him by about forty pounds. I also knew better than to ask him how he knew so much about taking care of patients or about how his good fences rule would work in this situation.

"Never believe that a few caring people can't change the world. For, indeed, that's all who ever have."

- Margaret Mead

Upon returning to school, I'd share my grandpa's wisdom with the other students who thought their friends back home were also getting dumber. I'd verse them on the finer points of patient and personal communication by telling them things like, **"They will never care how much you know until they know how much you care."** Interestingly enough, that exact statement has been shared hundreds if not thousands of times with my business and life coaching clients.

Have you ever been in a store and experienced a salesperson who knew every detail, fact, or statistic about a particular product you were going to purchase? In this case let's say that the information was more positive in favor of making this purchase and even better than you expected—yet you didn't make the purchase. This salesperson may have known all about the product, yet they made no concerned connection with you. I'll bet you have also been in a store just browsing and connected with a salesperson who immediately bonded with you. Next thing you knew, you had made a purchase. Maybe even a purchase that you hadn't planned on. Not only did you make the purchase, but you also felt good about that decision.

Oftentimes in public while I am being introduced to someone I don't know, one of the first questions that comes up is "What do you do for a living?" With great pride I proclaim, "I'm a chiropractor." Then they tell me about their back or neck pain, and next thing you know I have a new patient. It seemed everyone I met had health issues. Without even knowing it at the time, I was growing a practice faster than most doctors in my field. Within seven years, I had opened ten clinics, employed several doctors and staff members, and most importantly, we were helping a lot of people with their health issues. Many other chiropractors wanted to know my secret for success, so I started giving free seminars to our local doctors on patient care. When asked by many of these attendees about the real essence of what I was teaching, I realized I was teaching how to take care of people—the same care you would want your mother or any of your loved ones to receive. Doctors would tell me that it could not possibly be that simple. Soon I'd find myself upset that no matter how many times or how many different ways I would explain my theories of giving excellent patient care, I'd still hear them say, "It cannot be that simple!" I soon realized that giving excellent care was so simple to do that it was just as simple not to do. The key ingredient to excellent care for people was genuinely caring for them. Grandpa's idea proved itself to me over and over again throughout my life. **"They will never care how much you know until they know how much you care."** Everyone I've dealt with, whether in my business life or personal life, always knew I cared about them and for them.

CHAPTER 21

"It is better to give than to receive."

WHILE GRANDMA COULD share unconditional love with anyone at any time, Grandpa was much less likely to talk to strangers and certainly much less likely to give them anything. Remember, this is also the Grandpa who would tear up when commercials on TV would show starving children in third world countries, and he would immediately look at Grandma to start another donation. Grandpa had a way of using the quote **"It is better to give than to receive"** in a multitude of ways. I might ask for his advice and receive anything from a quick look to a full-blown lecture. You never knew exactly what Grandpa was going to share with you. The funny thing is no matter which way you received anything from him, he'd often follow it with **"It is better to give than to receive."** Imagine the joy of receiving amazing information from him, all the way to the fear of receiving Pete instead, then hearing that quote at the end of either delivery. Sometimes he was happy as heck and other times mad as hell.

Grandma's unconditional love was something every one of us should experience in our lives. She could give a stranger her last nickel and think nothing of it. If one of her family members needed anything, she'd do her best to make sure they received it even if it meant she might not eat for a few days. One time, years after Grandpa had passed, Grandma had lent out some of her food money to a relative. This led to her scraping her shelfs for food just so she could help out. Once I found out about it, it never happened again. Grandma and I spoke every Sunday no matter where I was or what I was doing. While having one of our weekly chats, I noticed a bit of despair in her voice. Further questioning led to her explaining a certain family member was having a tough financial time and she helped her out, which led to Grandma not having enough food money for a few days. That day I made it clear to all relatives who might put her in this situation that I would not stand for it. I also took over all of her finances, making sure she never wanted for anything.

> *"Remember that the happiest people are not those*
> *getting more, but those giving more."*
>
> *—H. Jackson Brown Jr.*

In the last chapter I discussed one of my longtime business partners, Mike, from our land development company. Mike was a firm believer of always making deals that, as he would say, left something on the table for the other guy. This was one of many great lessons I learned from this wonderful man. His theory was to be profitable but not to be overly greedy. He always said, "Leave something on the table for the other guy, and people will always want to do business with you." He felt by taking a fair profit from a project, we could still give a chance to the other guy. He believed as I do: **"It is better to give than to receive."** At the same time, we both thought it ridiculous to give without thinking of receiving. Running a business, we had to be profitable, but we knew we could also always be fair in all we did.

A huge part of my successes as a doctor, a father, a husband, a business consultant, and a land developer came from **"It is better to give than to receive."** Just about every time I made a decision in any of these categories, I'd always think about the other person's point of view. I would try my best to make the decision, direction, or deal more than fair to the others involved, because **"it is better to give than to receive."**

CHAPTER 22

"In matters of style swim with the current; in matters of principle stand like a rock."

MY GRANDPARENTS WERE absolutely as amazing as I could ever imagine two people ever being. Everything counted, everything mattered, and everything affected everything else. There was black or white, right or wrong, and never any gray area. I greatly appreciated this consistency and needed it in order to turn into a good, loving, serving, productive citizen. Come to think of it, the few times during my teen years when Pete jumped in to advance my learning curve, it was just as needed and appreciated.

When I was a teenager, bell bottom jeans were just starting to come into style, with the shirt of choice being a paisley button-down. In case that time in history is out of your memory's reach, allow me to explain this particular fashion. These jeans were tight on the hips and thighs and flared out wide below your knees, resembling a bell shape. To add to the allure, the bell bottom jeans carried a distinct swishing note when you walked due to the belled-out denim bottoms swooshing against each other. My grandpa found this design to be very peculiar to say the least. He'd often smirk and shake his head upon my entrance into a room while wearing this stylish outfit. Once while driving through town Grandpa pointed out some "hippies" who appeared to be smoking something other than cigarettes while wearing a similar outfit to mine. In an instant Grandpa said, "You're dressed like them. Does that mean smoking marijuana is next?" I declared, "No way, no sir, not ever! This was the style everyone was wearing, and drugs were a choice of people other than me!" He went on to say, "Good, you can wear your funny style, but you better not ever do drugs or else!" Funny as it seems today, I actually didn't answer back or experiment with drugs because of that one incident. Fear can be a powerful motivator. I bring this memory into this part of our lesson because later that day I heard for the first time what became one of Grandpa's all-time favorite quotes: **"In matters of style swim with the current; in matters of principle stand like a rock."**

> *"It is better to keep your mouth closed and let people think you are a fool than to open it and remove all doubt."*
>
> *- Mark Twain*

My grandparents were always meticulously clean and always dressed very respectably. Away from the home Grandpa always wore a suit with a stylish hat, and Grandma never left the house without a dress on, makeup perfect, and her amazing smile on as well. They would often say, "We may not have the best, but that doesn't keep us from acting, being, and looking our best." From time to time Grandpa would appear in a rather bold outfit only to be met by my confused look. I didn't have to say a word. Grandpa would handle that by saying, **"In matters of style swim with the current; in matters of principle stand like a rock.** And this, young man, is style." Again, who was I to argue with this wise man?

As was common during my short time with my amazing grandparents, I'd confuse the lessons. One such time I was driving (I had just received my driver's permit that week) around town with Grandma as my copilot. We approached a corner with a bunch of my friends standing around it, and I asked Grandma to quickly duck down so it would look like I was driving alone. Yes, I know now that showing off always comes back to bite us in the rump. As terrible as it sounds, Grandma did it and proceeded to get stuck in between the floorboard and the seat. If that wasn't bad enough, we both started laughing so hard we could barely breathe. In fact, we were both seconds away from peeing our pants. Let me correct that, me almost peeing my pants and Grandma almost peeing her dress. We were only two blocks from home, so we laughed our way to our driveway only to be met by Grandpa. The hollering started before I could even get out of the car. "Why in God's name are you driving my car alone? What is wrong with you? Are you stupid? Do you know that driving alone with only a permit is illegal? Where in the holy hell is your grandma?" All I could do was point to the floorboard, where Grandma was still stuck and still laughing hysterically. This is where the real genius of my grandma's joy shined. Grandpa ran around to her side of the car to rescue her from her predicament, and next thing you know we all three were laughing so hard, I was sure someone was going to pee their pants.

When we told Grandpa how she ended up on the floorboard of the car, I had to throw in my two cents and say, "We were sort of swimming with the current, Grandpa." Then the lesson was instilled in me again. He went on to rant about the differences between showing off and style, and somehow turned it into an issue of principle

—pretending to break the law by driving alone was a surefire way to become a criminal someday. He even went off on Grandma, saying, "Louise, if you don't teach the boy to stand for something, he'll fall for anything and be good for nothing." And of course, that led to me once again being told that I was bringing embarrassment to my grandparents, our family, and myself.

There is no way I could place a value on this lesson, or any of the lessons learned during my amazing time with my grandparents. All I can possibly say is thank you God, Grandma, Grandpa, and Pete. In honor of my grandpa and this particular rule, when we constructed our home in California, we had a six-foot-long by two-and-a-half-foot-high stone placed in our massive fireplace. On this stone was chiseled **"In matters of style swim with the current; in matters of principle stand like a rock."**

CHAPTER 23

"Finish what you start."

AS IT IS probably apparent to the reader by now, my grandparents, and quite possibly yours, lived by a few very simple rules. I say simple because if you live by these rules without wavering, your decisions and life will always be more amazing. If you practice these lessons daily, your life will be easy to enjoy, and prosperity will follow you.

This particular lesson was repeated to me so many times because of my wandering, creative (or destructive) daydreaming. I'd be doing homework and wander off on another thought without finishing the homework, and Grandma would catch me and refocus me with a quick **"Finish what you start."** I'd be washing their car and a thought of something needing repair on my dirt bike would appear in my daydreaming mind. Off I'd go to investigate the repair only to be halted and redirected from my secondary mission to my primary task by Grandpa. This redirection was usually stern and contained at least two **"Finish what you start"** statements, complemented with "If you ever plan on being anything, you have got to learn to **finish what you start.**" In school this could happen multiple times during a day. I could be writing the answer to a question and a bird would fly by the classroom window and off I'd go thinking I was Jonathan Livingston Seagull from the fantastic book written and published in 1976 by Richard Bach. It didn't take much for someone who cared about me in any way to say, **"Finish what you start."**

"Every person, all the events of your life are there because you have drawn them there. What you choose to do with them is up to you."

- Richard Bach

Today I say those same words to clients, my children, and myself dozens of times per week, if not dozens of times daily. Anytime I'm doing just about anything, I'll catch myself speeding up the completion of that particular task by saying, **"Finish what you start."** Then that often gets paired with **"Success loves action."** And of course, **"Anything worth doing is worth doing well."** Then when a flash of question enters my mind about dealing with others, I simply say to myself, **"Do unto others as you would want them to do unto you."** From time to time when fear of what could go wrong in any particular situation pops into my mind, I will remind myself that **"what you think about, you talk about, and eventually you bring about."**

With these few rules used in your day-to-day life, soon you will find yourself in charge of others, which will allow you to accomplish much more than you could ever accomplish by yourself. Could you imagine Henry Ford designing and eventually building each car by himself? How big would Ford Motor Company have grown if Mr. Ford didn't employ others? If you are going to grow beyond this point, you will have to adapt to the following rule. **"If you are going to expect anything from anyone, you must inspect everything from everyone."** As you train more and more people, you will have to demonstrate how important they are to the mission you are attempting to complete— anything from a neighborhood lemonade stand that is ready to expand to its second location, all the way to a major corporation expanding into another country. Everyone involved will have to be thinking about the company's reputation. After all, **"reputation, reputation, reputation—that's all you've got."**

Years ago, there was a study of quality control at a major automobile manufacturing company which disclosed that cars manufactured on Friday had the poorest quality ratings. The study revealed that Friday was the most missed day of the week at that factory, which meant the most substitute workers filling the roles of the absent employees. To turn this around, the manufacturers had to figure out how to make Fridays more enjoyable or they would have to utilize more robotics. You know what happened there. Within a few years there were more and more robots assembling cars and fewer and fewer workers. If the workers had applied a bit more pride in their product's reputation, there might have been a different path in the advancement of manufacturing.

"Common sense is not so common." We could easily continue to apply each Grandma and Grandpa rule to fill this chapter, but I'm hoping you will create the final chapters of your life by applying all the rules in this book. Soon your entire existence will improve, and our beautiful world will be a better place because you chose to live by a few amazingly simple rules.

We can make this world a better place by living by my grandparent's rules and accepting responsibility for all our actions and thoughts starting right now. From this moment on visualize and verbalize that you are expanding in all forms of abundance, prosperity, health, wealth, and love every day while inspiring others to do the same. Visualize, verbalize, and never compromise.

CHAPTER 24

A word about the brilliance of turning knowledge into wisdom.

WELL, WHAT DO you think? Having read these pages, is it possible that prior to reading this book you knew most of this Grandma and Grandpa wisdom for living a rich and healthy life? Is it possible you've heard this from your grandparents? Is it possible that you could take that knowledge and apply a bunch of positive action and live it? What would happen if today you and everyone you knew and everyone they knew started living from this commonsense model? What if people started treating people the same way they wished to be treated? Could you imagine how much more abundance, success, happiness, health, love, and prosperity would be all around us? By adopting and living by these simple rules, we could create a global impact, making this a far more beautiful world than it already is for our children and their children. Could you imagine how much happier, healthier, prosperous, and safer our world could become?

Neither you nor I can correctly answer that question until we have done it and lived it. And when we've done it and lived it and everyone, we know has done it and lived it, I believe this world will be a much better place. What do you believe? What is your perspective on this?

I'd like to share one brief story I heard years ago on the power of belief and perspective.

> *You see, a century ago two shoe companies each sent a salesperson to a third world country. These two salespeople traveled on the same ship and arrived at the same destination at the same time. Within twenty-four hours the first salesperson wrote a letter to his boss, declaring that the company's expansion into this country would be a disaster. "Stop all increased production! No one in this country wears shoes!" At the same time the other salesperson was also writing a letter for her boss. "Send more salespeople," she wrote, "and increase the factory to twenty-four-hour production. We've hit the jackpot. No one here wears shoes!"*

I dream of a day when common sense is common, and the normal way things are done. It's always the right way. Picture us loving, serving, and demonstrating excellence in all we do, and truly giving everything our all becomes the normal way of doing everything. Imagine a day when the true greatness of all our human potential is expressed daily for the good of all mankind.

> **"All I have seen teaches me to trust the Creator for all I have not seen."**
>
> **— Ralph Waldo Emerson**

The current selfishness demonstrated daily in our world bears witness that we need to demonstrate more common sense, happiness, love, and respect in all we do. I believe that the words shared in this book, when coupled with positive actions, could make a significant impact on improving everyone's life, health, and financial situation on our magnificent planet.

I have written this book for the world to help us all help ourselves make it a better place. I have written this book because I dream of a day when children can go to school or outside and learn and play safely. I have written this book in hopes of all of us respecting and thanking all of our amazing first responders. And as our youngest son, Tyden, who motivated me to write this book, prepares to go to the United States Marine Corps, I hope and pray for his safety and for a better and safer world for all.

I mainly wrote this book for you. I pray you take the necessary actions needed to facilitate amazing positive changes in your life. And as your life positively changes, please be sure to share this book with everyone who is important to you. Be sure to share it with everyone in your family, from your children, to your children's children, to your siblings, and certainly with your parents. Be sure to share it with all your friends, all your neighbors, all your coworkers, all your church members, and most certainly with all your social media friends. I believe that every man, woman, and child would be better off living the wisdom of my grandparents. If we know and live by these lessons, we can make our world a better place for our children's children. Who knows, global impact may be starting right now with you spreading this book of wisdom.

"The people who are crazy enough to think they can change the world are the ones who do."

- Rob Siltanen

"Pochissimo e necessario fare una vita felice; e tutto presso lei, nel vostro modo di pensare."

"Very little is needed to make a happy life; it is all within yourself, in your way of thinking."

— *Old Italian proverb*

CPSIA information can be obtained
at www.ICGtesting.com
Printed in the USA
LVHW050433300920
667478LV00005B/478